To Date a Man,
You Must Understand a Man:

The Keys to Catch a Great Guy
By Gregg Michaelsen

D1016467

To Date a Man, You Must Understand a Man:
The Keys to Catch a Great Guy

By Gregg Michaelsen
"Confidence Builder"

Copyright © 2014 Gregg Michaelsen

ISBN-13: 978-0692237243 (Gregg\Michaelsen)
ISBN-10: 0692237240

DISCLAIMER: As a male dating coach I am very good at what I do
because of my years of studying the nuances of interpersonal relationships. I have helped thousands of women understand men.

That said, I am not a psychologist, doctor or licensed professional.
So do not use my advice as a substitute if you need professional help.

Women tell me how much I have helped them and I truly hope that
I can HELP you too in your pursuit of that extraordinary man! I
will provide you with powerful tools. YOU need to bring me your
willingness to listen and CHANGE!

Congratulations on taking the first step to learning, understanding
and TAMING men!

Table of Contents

Intro to Understanding Men

What's most important to you in life beyond your health and your basic needs? The answer I get most often, and the one I choose, is relationships with the opposite sex. It amazes me how people go into them blind. They generally know what they want: an awesome lover, a family with three kids and the white picket fence. But they have no clue how to get there.

What is the result? Break-up after break-up and divorce after divorce.

Where is the manual that teaches women how to deal with men? Where is the detailed report on how to communicate with a man and get one's desires met? Where is the BOOK that gives you the KEYS to understanding the male mind?

And where is the course instructing women HOW to KEEP a man (who they love) in love with them?

Well, here it is.

Here is everything a woman needs to know to understand and not only survive her relationship, but FLOURISH!

My lady readers contact me over and over with their break-up stories and have asked me why my theories work. My answer so far has been, *"You don't need to understand the male mind just know that it works this way and follow my steps."*

I was wrong. Now I think you DO need to understand the male mind so you can help yourself out without me being there all the time for you.

This book will explain the MALE mind. And for every best seller I write, this book will NOW go along with it. This is **the Jewel** of all my books.

*GIVE a woman a man, he stays in love for a month. Show her how to UNDERSTAND a man, **they** stay in love for a lifetime…or something like that!*

Guys get away with tons of stuff in relationships and YOU allow them to! This book is going to strip men of their power and render them helpless UNTIL you have gained what you desire and then, and ONLY then, will we "power up" your man again.

Sounds pretty simple huh?

I mean, let's face it, love is not enough. I grew up thinking as long as you have love, you can get through anything, right? Bullshit. I get fifty emails a day from my lady readers and they consist of failed relationships based on outside factors like: long distance, in-law issues, children, health and aging, past relationship baggage, money, conflicting religious beliefs and lack of self-esteem to name a FEW!

Whoa! So no wonder we can't find our soul mate. You see we don't live in a vacuum. We all have baggage and outside influences. This makes knowing how to deal with men very important, so that this "baggage" can be handled without contempt being built from either party.

I had this Jewish girl contact me. She ended her seven year relationship because of her parent's influence. They would NOT accept her dating a non-Jewish man. Talk about outside influences!

This book is going to teach you all about the male mind so you can get the love you deserve, crave and need. By acquiring the blueprint to the male mind, we will then be able to handle all our baggage. I will show you how to get a man to reciprocate the love you hand out. No longer will your "all in" attitude get met with a lifeless, unemotional and non-committal couch potato wallowing in front of the football game.

Oh, this is going to be fun!

Men are simple creatures and, in general, we all think the same way. How do I know? Because thousands visit my website, KeysToSeductions.com, everyday! I know the male mind, have studied interpersonal relationships and I have the Best Sellers to prove it.

You see, you can't talk to a man like you talk to your girlfriends—and yet you do! Women bring their complicated emotions, nurturing and poor lack of timing right to their man and they get NOWHERE! Not only that, contempt builds and your guy is running off to spend more time with his friends golfing.

This dominoes and SNAP—you're single again and your self-esteem takes another blow.

Watch how magically we are going to get you communicating with men like they would communicate with each other. And at the root of this new communication will be the phrase, "catch me if you can!"

It doesn't matter how great you treat a man. If you don't learn his playbook, you will FAIL! What goes on inside his small brain, how he communicates and how he loves you will always be susceptible to emotional abuse and games.

I'm going to hand you the **Holy Grail** of communication with men. When an issue surfaces, we will shift you out of "emotional girl mode" and into what I call "man mode." Man mode is the state of mind where you can talk one-on-one with ANY guy and GET what you desire!

MAN MODE IS SIMPLY AWESOME AND IT WORKS!

And finally, *To Date a Man, You Must Understand a Man* is for all the young women out there seeking love for the first time. This book is for the women who are also in relationships and struggling to keep them together. This book is for our kids that will soon want true love and a family. And finally, this book is for all of us who get fed the useless crap in magazines, blogs and from our well-intentioned but wrong friends.

All women need to keep a copy of *To Date a Man, You Must Understand a Man* at their side and re-read it from time to time!

Now let's get to work!

Section 1
Understanding Men

 ## #1: The Conveyer Belt to Manhood

It makes me nauseous, and probably you too, to talk about hunting and gathering. Sorry, but men NEED to acquire things. Very important things. We are taught to get out there and drive a nice car, wear nice clothes, make tons of money and, yes, sleep with a lot of women.

Society plucks us from the womb and places us on the conveyer belt to manhood.

Think of us as a chocolate chip cookie getting cranked out at Chips Ahoy. Let's start with our ingredients: competition, challenge, self-worth, toughness and motivation to make money and provide. All this gets mixed into the batter that creates us.

Hot out of the oven, Dad quickly paints our room blue with tough animals on the wall and starts playing rough with us.

Before we can cool, we are climbing trees, learning to fight, strapped into skis and taught not to cry. Before long we are washing the car, bringing in the groceries, cutting the lawn and fixing the leaky sink. At fourteen, I was working at a local farm ripping out weeds that surrounded tomato plants for rubles an hour.

I remember that job. For the first time, even though I was making shit and was basically a part of forced child labor, I had a sense of worth and freedom. Sure, I had an allowance, but that was given to me. I didn't want things GIVEN to me. Well, I did, but I got more satisfaction with the pittance I got from pulling weeds.

No longer was I told by my parents what to do with my money. It was my money to blow on popsicles and bicycle parts.

It became increasingly evident that my manhood would be defined by what I do, how well I do it and how it compares to my peers. Like a monarch butterfly emerging from a chrysalis, STATUS was becoming the cornerstone of my universe. With status comes confidence and with confidence came a man that could begin to understand the world and LOVE.

Money became important.

Today, I see relationships that fall apart because a man has no self-worth or confidence. You see, some men fall off the conveyer belt early and are placed in the "reject" pile. This usually has a lot to do with a guy not being able to provide. He can't get a job or his job is very low paying and/or brings no status.

I know this sounds shallow, but it's how we are internally wired. Guys turn to drugs and alcohol when they feel they don't "measure up" to their peers or parents' expectations. They emotionally, and sometimes physically, abuse women. Or they feel the need to sleep with as many women as possible to PROVE their self-worth. This proves to be a failing endeavor.

Other "rejects" are men that never had a fighting chance. They grew up without a dad or older brother. Or their parents were drug addicts or alcoholics. Maybe they couldn't get out of the hood and were forced to join gangs on the east side.

Of course, this leads to a path of sadness, depression and loneliness.

And guess what? Many women pick these types of men and don't even know it!

We are PROVIDERS. That is our DNA makeup. Money is more important to us than women realize. If we can't pay the rent, afford a car or afford to put food on the table, how can we ever measure up to ourselves and YOU?

A man must complete his mission of manhood by becoming self-reliant and this is defined by who he is, how much he makes and how he is defined by the important people in his life.

Until he becomes self-reliant, women will not and should not be a focus in his life.

But they are.

Sure, he might say that he loves you and he wants to eventually marry you, but in his mind YOU are dispensable until he has a better definition of the man he is in life. He himself might not be aware of this very set of facts. We are providers and we must provide for the people we love and our future offspring. If we can't, then we feel like failures.

To prove this point, I am bombarded everyday with emails like this one:

> *"Gregg, Jim and I have been together for 4 years. I supported him through most of this time. I was there for him while he went back to college. I gave it my all. Finally, he landed a great job, and about this time he said he doesn't love me anymore. I am heartbroken, this is my future man. PLEASE HELP!"*

See how this affects you? Until a man can DEFINE himself, YOU are secondary. I'm sorry this is the case, but until you understand this, you will continue to FAIL with men.

You could stop right here, digest what I just stated, never pick a man like this ever again and you will CHANGE YOUR LIFE for the better!

Many girls love their man unconditionally and can't understand why their guy won't reciprocate. "Sex is great and my Mom loves him," they say.

Money is not important (I'm ruling out gold diggers here) to a lot of women. Most girls live a life of scarcity, so when a weak man arrives at her door she invites him in like a wet kitten. If she has money, then what's the problem?

What's the problem? The problem is he is a wet kitten! Then women try to "mold" this man into greatness. They don't understand that this is IMPOSSIBLE for any length of time. This wet kitten needs to go back outside and grow into a lion and YOU cannot do it for him. Instead, you let him inside to piss on the rug for months and years. And before you know it, you are thirty-nine years old, desperate for kids and single.

Now there are exceptions to everything. If a twenty-year-old is on his way to completing his engineering degree or a guy is nearing the end of a vocational school course to be a car mechanic, they know that their realization to provide is close to fruition. These men might be ready to love a woman.

I'm here to tell you that you need to choose men and not be chosen. There are millions of wet kittens out there BUT there are millions of full grown lions out there too. For you to experience love you need to PICK from the full-grown lion bin!

But there is a catch. The full-grown lions don't patronize the usual watering holes. Very few "Mufasas" (let's stick with *The Lion King* theme here) are bar flies hanging out on a Saturday night. You see, they don't need to chase women.

THEY ATTRACT WOMEN EVERYWHERE THEY GO.

Also, lions are choosers too. They want interesting, motivated, high-value women. Women with integrity and boundaries. Women that know what THEY want in life and in a man.

I will make you this woman!

Some points to remember:

- So now we understand the influences that society brings to a man. We understand the ingredients that become our make-up or DNA if you will. These include competition, challenge, self-worth, toughness and motivation to make money and provide.

- Money brings us status and is VERY important to ALL men even though it is NOT necessarily important to you.

- How we are viewed by others (mainly male role models) correlates directly with our self-esteem.

- We are not able to love ourselves or women until we have attained what we consider success.

- Women tend to date "wet kittens" because they feel they can change them. They can't. They piss on the rug, go out and never come back.

- "Lions" don't hang out at the usual watering holes. They are choosers too, just like you will be soon!

#2: We Love in Different Ways

In this chapter we need to understand how men and women differ when it comes to love. Once we understand the differences, we can allow each other to love in our "proper" ways.

A woman's love is a sight to behold! Her emotions bubble to the top for all to see. She is happy and complete in life. Her man's decisions are supported, successes are celebrated and even failures are smoothed over. Nothing, nothing comes between her and her man.

She listens and wants to hear all about your day. Even when her guy treats her like trash, she is still there, maybe even blaming herself for the treatment. Over and over she goes all in to make the relationship work. Sex is granted and her love is unconditional!

Her love makes sense to her and, case after case, it AMAZES me!

I think this is the very reason why I have switched to helping women today. I see this and it makes me cry. You contact me, you ooze love, but you are totally broken. It frustrates me to my core to have the answers for you and not be able to have a big enough platform to tell ALL women. I guess this is why I always give away so many free books.

One problem though, men don't love like this. Women expect a man to love back in the same way. They want to see emotions spilled out after work and flowers once a week to confirm their love. Women want communication after making love. She wants him to love babies, cry, cook, clean and show his vulnerable side.

I'm sorry, but it's NEVER going to happen. We love in a different way. Now I'm not saying we can't love in some of the ways you do. No. I'm saying, in general, we love in a consistent way, but VERY differently.

Back to our conveyer belt. We are taught to hide our emotions, remember? From day one the crying must stop. It's not natural for us to express our emotions every hour. Thus, you are not going to hear, "I love you" twice a day unless we are some lame wimpy-ass guy. We don't want to change diapers, not because we are lazy, but because we are taught this is not a "man's job."

We want to fix the lawnmower, shovel the snow and carry the groceries in. Many men don't even know why they like these chores because they don't understand themselves or the "conveyer belt to manhood." They just understand that they NEED to do these things to please and provide for their girl and children. It makes them FEEL good. It is his DNA speaking.

And if we feel good about ourselves, then we can love.

Sexist? Fuck, yes. But true. I am not here to sugarcoat the male mind or make excuses. Agree or disagree, it is your choice. Fight against what I am telling you and YOU will wind up on the losing side.

But embrace and understand what I am saying AND use it to YOUR full advantage and YOU will change your life!

Now remember, just because we love in different ways doesn't mean we can't change diapers, wash clothes or cook meals. So please don't send me the hate mail!

We can. In fact, if we are "complete men" we want to do ALL these things. My point is that many women force their guy to do these things and take away the duties that we NEED to do because they don't understand the male mind.

If you constantly make the plans for the evening, tell us what we are doing wrong in the bedroom, dress us AND expect us to change the diapers, you will make us impotent and slowly destroy our self-worth.

Destroy our self-worth and you destroy the relationship!

You must let us be MEN. Even if YOU are the boss in the relationship. Let us take out the garbage and make the plans at times. Let us wear that stupid shirt. Humor us and say that we are great lovers in the bedroom and "steer" us to being a great lover: "Gregg, that feels awesome, now go just a bit slower."

Am I making sense?

How Men Love

We will say "I love you" in OUR way! Our way consists of ACTIONS:

1) Solving your problems

I know this sounds very unromantic, but it's true. We give you a back rub when your back aches. We stay up with you when you can't sleep. If we love you, we start paying for things because we are providers. It doesn't matter if you don't need us to pay. We will fix your car or get your car to a mechanic that will. Household issues? We're on it! Cutting the lawn, building a shed or changing out the kitchen cabinets let us show you our love through actions.

When you say, "The lawn looks great, honey, can you do the backyard too?" We want to cum our pants! Then, we want to do MORE things for you. Backyard? Done.

"Gregg, it can't be that simple."

YES IT CAN! AND IT IS! We are that simple. Keep a tasty treat above our jowls and we will do the trick over and over.

Or do it YOUR way:

"I thought you said you were going to cut the back yard too. You never finish anything you start."

Ugh. We go limp, fetal and head to the couch with a beer. Backyard? Fuck that.

Your choice. But only one of the ways above hits our love language button.

You see, this is how we feel and show love. We do silly "manly" things for women. Granted, cutting the lawn is not as romantic as flowers, but believe me it will lead to flowers if you compliment us on our duties.

Are you getting this? So the next time a guy or your guy fixes something for you or does a favor, he might be saying, "I love you." As silly as this may sound to you, you need to realize this. If you don't, contempt will build on both sides and chip away at the relationship bit by bit.

And often times, a man will say, "I love you," because you are making him. He figures it is easier just to say it when he doesn't necessarily mean it.

Ultimately, the words will flow out of his mouth but they need to come out naturally.

2) Protecting you

I always tell women to look for chivalry. This trait is POWERFUL. If a man opens doors, walks next to you against the traffic and helps you sit down at a restaurant...he LOVES you! He will defend you at all costs too. In a dark alley walking to the car, we are in protection mode for you. It's built in to our DNA. Again, it's not as romantic as saying, "I love you", but it is OUR way.

3) Socially announcing you

This is huge. If we post FB photos of you—then you have us hooked. When we are HAPPY to meet your Mom, friends and ATTEND your hobbies, we are hooked. When we WANT you to meet OUR Mom, friends and attend our hobbies, again, we are SHOWING you that we are in LOVE!

When we put our friends on the back burner? WOW, we are in love. Look for this. When a man socially announces you to the important people in his life, he is showing you that he truly loves you. Look for it. And if you don't see this in your man, then move on.

4) Taking on Responsibility

Another big one. When a man helps you with boring

stuff, he is probably starting to fall in love with you. Let's face it, moving your furniture to a new apartment is no fun for any man. Bringing you soup when your breath stinks and your make-up is all over the place because you are sick with the flu means we love you. Or staying home from work to help you with a project. All of these are positive signs of a guy showing you his love.

Buying a car and the salesman is treating you like shit? Watch as we take control, waste that salesman and get you that car cheap.

Mmmmm—watch as Tarzan take on salesman!

5) Sex
Big subject, ladies. Back when we were growing up, one of our most coveted "rites of passage" was to have sex with as many women as possible. Maybe this is the caveman reproduction thing, who the fuck knows. But somewhere, we got judged, and our status stamped by our male peers based on how many women we could have sex with.

I am not proud of this male fact. And I'm sure, right now, you aren't proud of me. But it is true. In fact, of all our achievements, I think sex ruled us the most in our late adolescent/early adult years. We would lie all the time to our friends and tell them we slept with girls even if we didn't. We would pray that they would not find out. I now know that they were all lying back to me as well.

My point is that being proficient at sex has stuck to all men. We need to believe that we are good at it. So this affects you directly. You need to be gentle with our feelings. More gentle than you think.

Say, "I love that, now slow down with your tongue."

Don't say, "Ow! That hurts, haven't you ever done this before?"

Ouch.

Remember, men THINK they are great in the sack. In reality, most of us suck. Shit, I didn't know the difference between an asshole and a clit until I was 22.

But DON'T tell us we suck! Teach us slowly and with great sensitivity to our little boy feelings, and watch how good we can become. When we get good at sex, then we want to satisfy you more. And let's face it, all women are very different when it comes to pleasure and orgasms.

So many women get angry at their guy for not "trying harder" when we have no fucking idea what you want because we are afraid to ask. This deflates our manhood and our dicks!

So understand this point and talk about it with your guy and things will stay HOT in the bedroom. It's just another one of our differences in showing love.

Now, obviously, there are exceptions. Some guys rock in the bedroom. But don't assume this.

When we want sex all the time, we are hooked. Look for this and keep an eye on it. One of the first things I ask a woman (to her shock and horror) is how often does she have sex with this guy. When I hear barely once a week, there is a problem.

Men need sex often but we don't always want a long

drawn out session. Understand this. If you come with an owner's manual on "how to get you off" and it involves 3 chimpanzees and an albino midget riding a bike—we are going elsewhere. This could be You Porn or another woman but understand this is HOW we are.

That said, we WANT and NEED to please you. Communicate with us in a positive way and we will be more than happy to reciprocate. We know we can't "just get off" all the time without pleasing you. But allow us before work, maybe, to get rough and selfish without the dreaded speech of your sexual needs not being met in every session. This is HUGE.

Let's face it, we can stare at a glass of milk and get off. You, on the other hand, need much more emotion and foreplay. So the reality is we are going to get off much more than you. It's ok!

Let us and don't fall into the justice trap of "you orgasmed, so I need to."

We will reciprocate. Show us how, but dumb it down and be gentle with our feelings.

Some caveats to understanding how we love:

- Sometimes a man, especially a PUA (Pick Up Artist), will "fake" these qualities above because he just wants to do the horizontal mambo. If you are hot, he will survive on sex for a while. He can easily fake chivalry on the first couple of dates until he gets what he wants.

- Look for "protecting you" and "socially announcing you", these are rarely faked. Also, most men won't throw a lot of cash towards a relationship. If he spends a lot of money on you, then he is usually into you. Rich guys won't care, but there are fewer of these types out there.

Remember, we are just trying to understand men in this section. Later, in "Your New Game Plan", we will show you exactly how to know if a man loves you or if he is an asshole stringing you along!

So ladies, we love in different ways. We might not want to go shoe shopping with you at the mall, but we love how those shoes look on you. We want to take you in those shoes to the party and show you off. We might even want to pay for those shoes, although you don't NEED us to pay or you didn't even ask.

We might not want to talk about our day to you when we get home but it's not because we don't love you. It's because we need to mentally retreat, regroup and then we will be happy to talk about our day and yours.

And sometimes we just need to "get off" without emotion. It's ok, we still love you and we will love you even more if you stop making us feel guilty about it. This is a big reason sex falls off. We sometimes cower at the thought of not pleasing you, so we make excuses for not having sex. This is especially important with the rise of porn today. I am seeing more and more relationship failures because men are able to hit the porn site and forego an emotional relationship with their partner. They head to the land of virtual sex where all is good and no women exist.

If you understand how a man loves and how you love, then you start to see the light. No longer will you go into panic mode and worry about the relationship. Instead, you talk to your girlfriends when we are not emotionally available and wait for us to come to you.

#3: How Men Determine a Keeper

This chapter explains how men determine a "keeper", a woman that we will commit to versus the girls that we date a few times and move on. Let's call these two types: "rest stops" and "keepers".

Rest Stops

No, I'm not talking about pole dancers or total party girls that just want to get laid. Although these types do fit into this category. I'm talking about women that set very few boundaries or have little respect for themselves when it relates to men. They might be intelligent, independent and attractive but when it comes to a guy, they have no clue.

This type of woman says yes to men. She doesn't know what type of guy she wants or even what she wants out of life with a man. She just knows she wants to be happy. Maybe get married and have some kids. She is pretty much ready to have sex whenever a man shows interest. She feels if she says no, then the guy will move on to another woman.

I find this interesting because women are so choosey with so many things: the clothes you wear, your hair stylist and, of course, your shoes. But men?

So if you are always being chosen and not choosing guys, how are you going find love? By accident? Maybe the guy that chooses you, without YOU giving any resistance, will happen to be a great guy?

I doubt it.

This is NOT some far out example. Many women fit into this category and they don't even realize it. They have no idea what SPECIFICALLY they want in a guy.

They sleep with men too early. They say yes to the date no matter where it is or how soon it comes up. This doesn't necessarily make them sluts. They just have low self-esteem and, therefore, they have limited choices when it comes to men.

Now, many men love this type of woman, albeit for a few weeks. But there is no challenge here. Any guy can have this type of girl so there is no competition to get her. Her time is not valuable and she probably has limited career aspirations. She simply is not attractive because she is not a challenge and she has no boundaries.

Keepers

I can spot keepers right out of the gate because I'm a dating coach. But for most men, they start noticing a keeper when she starts talking. Keepers wield POWER. This woman knows what she wants in a man. Her time is valuable and the "game" is a joke to her.

Her body language screams keeper also. She controls the "dance", if you will. Guys will walk up to her and she will be very polite and even appreciate the advance. But right off the bat, SHE decides a guy's fate. She CHOOSES men—she is not CHOSEN.

Pick up artists need not apply!

She has boundaries. And she SETS them. She will not hand over her phone number easily and she will nicely exit a situation where a "little boy" is trying to get into her pants. It's actually fun to witness a PUA around a woman of this stature. She doesn't show her cleavage like other girls do. No, not at this stage.

Her time is valuable because she has passions, which make her time valuable by default. Why would she date some loser when she can be with other men of quality who she sees on a daily basis?

How quality men define a keeper:

Conversations are deeper. This girl will not be talking about the weather. She has an interesting life to share with other interesting people. She has MANY experiences under her belt and she is looking for more. She will tire of a shallow man quickly. One liners are sad to her.

She will ask you pointed questions. If a guy approaches her, or she approaches a guy (which she will), she will ask questions that are instant qualifiers. "Tell me, Gregg, why do you want to take me out? You don't even know who I am." or "Gregg, I heard what you said over there, please expand on that thought. I found it interesting."

She will never run over and scream, "Hey, wanna do a shot?"

She sets boundaries immediately. If asked for her number, she will respond kindly, "I don't give it out to guys I just met. Give me yours and maybe I'll contact you." If you are lucky enough to make the cut and go out with her, she won't offer up sex for weeks, maybe months. She

KNOWS what she wants in a man and she demands to be treated in a certain way. And until he proves his worth, her pussy is in lock-down mode. She has options.

Her radar is set to max. Think a guy is going to play her? Think again. She knows the game of love and she already knows what I am teaching you right now.

Only quality men need apply. Now, you may think this woman is a bitch. Quite the contrary. Guys are IN-STANTLY attracted to this woman. Many will cower and go fetal, but this is her whole point. She weeds out the runts and attracts only quality men. When I train men, I bring them around women of this nature and I show them how far away they are from finding true love. Not to discourage them, mind you, but to show them that this is what they need to work at attaining.

You see, what I am describing above is POUNDED into you by all my books:

Men seek women of VALUE. They bring us happiness. They keep us engaged. They satisfy all the man ingredients that are instilled in us. A woman of value keeps our eyes from wandering and always keeps us challenged. We want to and can grow with this type of girl. If we get out of line, she will leave us! She will always be worthy of a high-value man, so we will constantly be fighting to prove our worth.

These are the girls that we bring home to show Mom and show off to our friends! These are the women that we MARRY and have kids with.

*I am going to make you into this woman
if you are not already!*

#4: What Men Require

Ok, you are doing great. A couple more chapters and then we are going to whip you into shape with some life-altering activities (your new playbook) to attract any single man. And most married men too. :)

Here we need to examine what men require to stay committed to you. Remember, we are very simple creatures so you will easily understand this stuff. Just don't FORGET these requirements. I teach women to repeat them every morning when they are in a relationship—it's MAGICAL and it's SIMPLE.

1) Make us feel special

2) Let us be in control

3) Stand by our side

Make Us Feel Special

It is imperative that men feel special in the eyes of their women. A man needs to feel that he is the only one that she could be with. This means even if we are not, make it clear that we are. Remember how competition is one of our main ingredients? Use it to your advantage and make it clear that we are the ONLY man that you could be with. Make us feel worthy.

Make us feel like we have BEAT all other men and proudly display it!

This makes us run around the ball field screaming, "I win, I win, I win." Next, it locks us down and MAKES us want to KEEP winning. Now, don't worship us, just keep us knowing that, for now, we are doing good.

If you demean us in front of other people or you have a close male friend that you share private stuff with, this will sabotage the relationship. This touches on jealousy a little bit but this is not what I'm going for. This is about self-worth. If we feel like we have conquered other men, which is our goal from birth, then we will fight to keep that going. It's like we are defending our castle with a moat and alligators. I told you we are simple creatures, ha!

This doesn't mean you roll over and make him your hobby. You still need to keep a challenge going at times and change one thing every week. (This is a whole chapter coming up.) Remember, none of my tips happen in a vacuum, they ALL need to gel together. Do this and you will be a content girl.

Let Us Be in Control

So maybe you make more money than us and you don't need us to buy you dinner every time, but LET us if we want to! Maybe you are a DIYer around the house, but let us fix the sink or shovel the driveway. We are built for manual labor, so let us do manual labor. Let us fix things or try to fix things even if we break more stuff than we fix. Even though we know you can open your own door, let us open it for you if we want to. Smile and say, "Thank you, dear. That was thoughtful."

Humor us in all phases. You can even wear the shoes in the relationship but still give up control every now and then. Phrase things to us in this way:

"Where do you want to go to dinner? The Tavern on the Green?"

You know where you want to go but you didn't emasculate us by saying no to our idea. You just "steered" us to your choice.

I know you are scratching your head saying, "Ok, I know you said men are simple, but really? This is all I have to do keep a man?"

REALLY!

I wish you could pop inside my brain for a day. You would pop back out and probably turn lesbian. Kidding. But you would have an epiphany! You would pop back out and say, "OMG, men REALLY are that simple!"

Then you would run around the ball park screaming, "I win, I win, I win."

You see women have collaborated around the world and decided we are too complicated to figure out, so why try, just give up. I'm here to tell you that we are THAT SIMPLE. We require a little food, water, sex and we are good!

Always Stand by Us

Even when we are wrong, you must stand by us. You must side with us even if your family and friends say otherwise. This can sometimes be a very hard thing to do. But if you break this pact, we will leave you. Now, obviously if we purposely run over a dog, you will not support us, but you are dating a quality man now and quality men do not purposely run over a dog.

This comes down to being loyal also. The worst thing you can ever do is have an affair. Most men will never recover. Now, I know something is very wrong for you to have an affair but this is the ultimate insult to a man who is in love. This kills our self-worth.

We need to know that you are always there when we come home or need you. Many men give up their friends for their wife and family, so their world becomes very one dimensional.

#5: Why Did He Leave Me? The Five Mistakes

In this chapter I am going to run through a typical scenario that MILLIONS of women have experienced.

I put this in my "Understanding Men" section for a reason. I want you to understand how a man reacts in conjunction with what you do. Later, I will take these five mistakes and show you EXACTLY how to counter your mistakes in the section: "Your New Game Plan."

After this chapter you are going to have another epiphany that just might change your life!

Have you ever been in a relationship so intense that you said, "This is the man I am going to marry"?

You know what I'm talking about. Your heart raced every time the text came in and you saw his name. Butterflies flew around your stomach two hours before your date.

When together, your knees went weak. He was great-looking and romantic. He opened doors for you and seemed to protect you. Your friends admired him and you talked to your Mom about this great guy.

You started thinking about your future together. The house, the kids and the two golden retrievers.

You envisioned holidays together and trips to Disney.

And why not? He said ALL the right things. He told you he loved you and he loved kids. He whispered into your ear how sexy you were and how he can't wait to get you under the sheets. He talked about taking you to Saint

Bart's for an exotic vacation.

THEN, OUT OF NOWHERE, HE WAS GONE.

The texts stopped coming. The plans got broken. And then the excuses started piling up.

At first, you gave him the benefit of the doubt. Ok, his job is crazy or he has family issues.

Crickets.

Now you probably made a few futile attempts to contact him to see if everything was ok. He might have responded with, "I'll contact you in a couple of days."

But you knew he wouldn't…and he didn't.

Then you started asking, "What did I do wrong?" You began running through the scenarios over and over again until you got obsessed with the situation. All the time you are elevating this man to an even higher status. Shit, by the time you contact me this guy is Zeus!

So he exited your life in one of two ways: the "drip-drip method" or the "sudden cut-off" method. Either way, the result is the same – HE IS GONE!

Next, your friends tell you to move on. They TRY to soothe you with stuff that doesn't work. You go out on a date and all you do is compare this loser to your Zeus… the poor bastard.

"No one compares to my Zeus."

The bummer is your ego has taken another hit. You build contempt for men, and I don't blame you. But this has a very negative impact moving forward. The next guy will be another wet kitten, but this time a WETTER kitten! The pendulum swings and you get hurt again.

The funny thing is you know you are smart and sexy. You know that you are strong and you know you are a catch. But you just don't understand the puzzle to a man's mind. If only you did?

The bottom line? There is no course in life on this subject. Just shitty magazines telling you false crap about finding and keeping a man with the latest in make-up and lipo.

Stop obsessing about your past and start UNDERSTANDING men!

How? By listening to a man! Forget listening to your Mom, your shrink and your friends and let's get REAL.

This is why he left you:

MISTAKE #1: You were not a challenge

You have money, good looks, you treated him like gold and you are extremely intelligent. That's great, but that is secondary.

You were not a challenge! You were all in and he knew it. You got a checkmark next to your name because he conquered you and then he moved to the next girl. You did what came naturally to you. I understand and I am not blaming you. But what YOU need and what HE needs are two VERY different things.

Our conveyer belt of manhood taught us competition and challenge, remember? Provide that to us and we will NEVER leave you. I will solve this later in this book but for now I want YOU to understand why he left you.

MISTAKE #2: Too much pursuit too soon

Guys need to take control. We ask girls out. We decide where to go. We control sex (we actually don't, but more on that later.) We propose. We solve problems!

Reverse this and our brains short out and smoke pours out of our ears!

This is not to be confused with asking him out at the beginning. And I'm not saying that you can't take control sometimes. No. But there is a way to do this that keeps us in control. Sometimes we just think we are in control and you fooled us but that's ok…just LEARN how to fool us!

This book will teach you how.

Again, this goes back to our roots—our conveyer belt of manhood. Nowhere were we taught to be controlled by a woman other than our Mom. I am not being a chauvinist here, I am telling you HOW we are wired. You can fight me and listen to your girlfriends or you can EMBRACE this concept and SOLVE men from the ground up.

Here are some examples of over-pursuit:

- You remind us how great last night was

- You make reservations at our favorite restaurant "as a surprise" to us on Saturday Night

- When we don't contact you for a day you ask us if everything is ok

- You start talking and/or planning about our future together on a regular basis

- You start to dress us and explain what is best for us on a day-to-day basis

Now, again, I understand this comes naturally to you. Your conveyer belt spits you out to nurture and love. So everything you do towards us makes sense to you. But you need to save this nurturing for your kids. And use it sparingly towards your man, especially in the early stages of a relationship.

A guy needs to pursue and you are pursing him instead. You, in his eyes, are acting clingy and needy.

Step back, be in and out of being aloof and let us do our thing.

If you keep pushing us towards our future with you in the form of planning dates and "seeing where we are headed", WE will head out the door.

You can pursue a little bit but then back off.

MISTAKE #3: You hold us in contempt

This is an interesting one and it needs to be discussed. Many women have been burned so many times that they are just plain bitter at the guys they meet.

They break out the checklist:

- He's too smooth with the lines

- He dresses way too nice, he must be a PUA

- He dresses like a slob, he's broke

- He's older, he must be married

- He's younger, he isn't mature

Next, if we pass these first tests, we are subjected to more torture. The next checklist, about kids and our future together, gets inserted before the second date. You are thinking you won't waste your time on an emotionally unavailable guy again, so let's get to the point quick so you don't waste your time.

The problem is you don't give men the time to express themselves about what they WANT and NEED.

We also pick up on this "contempt vibe" you are sending out and it is NOT attractive. We have "feelers" too, and we know almost immediately that you are bitter towards men. This tells us that you have been rejected and we start wondering why and what is wrong with you.

We don't necessarily want to hurt you. We are like you, we are trying to figure out love and what makes us happy too. And often times your (and our) past relationships get in the way.

I have the solution to your contempt problem. I will give you that "checklist" so you won't waste your time, but he will NOT be aware of it. *Hint:* By pushing him towards scheduling a day date with you, you lose a lot of the bullshitters out there. More on that later.

MISTAKE #4: You made him your hobby

This applies to a lot of women who are in a relationship. Women tend to drop all their ambitions and their friends and instead concentrate all their energy on a man.

NO, NO and NO! Challenge dies, pursuit increases and contempt builds. This is so easy to fix! Never make a man your hobby. Instead, join in his hobbies, pursue your own and ALWAYS keep a social network outside of his!

Please, ladies, this is one of the most common and most preventable mistakes I see. This kills the challenge and forces us into places you don't want us to be. We also don't know how to discuss this with you: *"Honey, will you go find some friends or hobbies to do without me?"*

Yeah, that will go over well!

Again your conveyer belt says, love and nurture but you must fight this.

MISTAKE #5: You gave us sex too soon

Encyclopedias are written on this subject. "Get it over with." "Thirty-day rule." "Sixty-day rule." "Ninety-day fucking rule."

As a woman, you have powers.

USE THE POWER OF THE PUSSY!

Here is your rule:

__DEFINE__ what you must have in a man. __DECIDE__ how you must be treated by a man. When this man __PROVES__ to you through multiple __ACTIONS__ that he is treating you the way you want to be treated, __THEN__, and __ONLY THEN__, do you have sex with him.

Actions. Not words. Not "I love you." Anyone can say shit but few can follow through. Don't tell me that you are worried about losing him if you delay sex. Are you kidding me? If you lose him because you didn't have sex, then he just wanted you for sex!! That is such a pitiful statement. You are a woman of worth, not a sex toy. Don't let a guy prey on your emotions.

So, you see, time is not the deciding factor here. Proof by actions are. Now, I highly doubt that he can prove himself in two weeks. He can't. So you may be into the thirty- to ninety-day category. Just be sure.

Guys will do anything to get into your hoop. They will lie, buy you shit, meet Mom and go to extremes to conquer you. YOU need to use your intuition, family and friends to determine if this guy is full of shit or not.

Later I will you show exactly what type of dates to go on to expose men for their true intentions.

Now I am not saying give up all your inbred female emotions just to please us, no. I am saying BALANCE your emotions and be AWARE of these five mistakes so he will never leave you. If you sense he is getting bored, READ over the five mistakes, realize which one (or all) you are doing and TAKE action!

Section 2
Your New Game Plan

 #6: Emotion Control: Act Like a Guy

We must do a chapter on emotions. I cover this a little bit in the "Man Mode" chapter (next) but we need more.

You have your powers: your mind, your legs, your ass, your breasts and, of course, your hoop (for lack of a better word). But you have a GLARING weakness—your emotions!

It's like you have massive armor plates all around your body but one glaring target on your back with a bright red sign that says, "Shoot here if you want to control me."

Smart men (assholes) see this target and know how to take aim and abuse your emotions. They know how to get exactly what they want out of you. Maybe it's sex or money or maybe they want to mooch off you for three months until they can find someone new.

Then, to add insult, they spin everything upside down and blame YOU! I hear it all the time. Post-breakup, the woman wonders what SHE did wrong and whether she can do things better—if only she can get him back.

Dumbass men know how to take advantage of your emotions too, and they don't even know what the hell they are doing…they just stumble over it.

"Lookee what dumbass can do!"

From this day forward you need to gain control over your emotions when it comes to men. This is MOST important at the beginning and at the end of a relationship.

I know, I know, this isn't a popular subject, but we have to talk about it.

Excessive emotions don't work with us. They get you nowhere at best and they can ruin your whole relationship at their worst. Don't make them disappear. You can't. Just HIDE them from us. Count to ten, walk away or call your best girlfriend. She will listen and she will understand—we will cower, go fetal and run.

Now, I'm not judging you. Your emotions help you in many ways. You need them to be a great mother and to be all in when it comes to love. Commitment issues will almost never be a problem if you find the right guy. I admire this quality, as do many men.

But your emotions can control your actions and that is NOT good when it comes to men. If a man is abusive, your emotions may say, "I need to try harder" or "it's my fault because I wasn't there for him when he needed me."

That's crap. The REAL answer is to get the fuck away from this abusive asshole and find a REAL man.

But that is your mind speaking. And that is how a man thinks. You make decisions based upon emotions and I am asking you to be aware of this and switch to the proper setting sometimes – Man Mode.

The best way is to prove it to yourself. When you feel you are getting emotional with a guy you love do this:

- Recognize it first (obviously)

- Stop and ask yourself, "What would he do?" or "What is he about to do?"

- Then do it to him first!

Sounds weird, right? But try it. Walk away. Stop talking to him just like he is about to stop talking to you. Turn away just like he is about to do to you. Walk out of the house. Call your friends. Go join your friends. This is your mind at work, not your emotions.

I know it sounds counter-productive, but to the contrary, it is very effective. Why?

- Because you are communicating just like he communicates to his friends, so he understands and responds to this.

- Your lack of communication will shock him because he is expecting you to bitch and whine (be emotional).

- Then SNAP—he realizes something is really wrong here and now HE wants to communicate with you!

And this comes back to my saying,

When in doubt, act like a guy.

Care less. Guys never care about minor things—you do. Women analyze every little scrap of emotion men let out. Why? Because we don't let out much, so when we do it's important to you. **Act like a guy.** Let out very little yourself as if YOU care less. Suddenly, guys will want more because you become mysterious. When you act like an emotional woman, we become immune to all your emotions and we stop listening.

Don't show him that you are emotionally involved. Let him do that. Guys hide their emotions (remember the conveyer belt to manhood?), so do the same. **Act like a guy.** Never say, "I love you" first. Let him. Never say, "We need to talk." Let him. His emotions are there, they just don't appear until he knows you are the woman for him…so let him find that out without you trying to advance the relationship. It works and it's MAGICAL!

Treating you badly? Leave him. A guy will not put up with being mistreated. If you have an affair, he will leave you. If you treat him like dirt, he will leave you. **Act like a guy.** If his actions and your intuition say leave him—LEAVE HIM! Women take all kinds of crap. Emotional or even physical abuse takes place and they come back for more.

Don't try to FIX him. I stated this earlier about taking in wet kittens. Men don't try to fix women, they dump them and try to find a woman of higher quality. **Act like a man.** When you realize that this man is "broken", which should be on the first date—dump his ass! "I need money", "I need a place to live until I get on my feet." SCREW THAT. You want to attract "lions" who are not broken. Lions are quality guys that have confidence and are seeking YOU, if you are of quality. This book will make you quality.

Show off and buy guy toys. Men buy fast cars, tough dogs and expensive sunglasses because it makes them feel confident, worthy and it attracts women. **Act like a guy.** Put on your Oakleys, buy a fast convertible car and have your pit-bull ride shotgun! I'm serious. If you can afford it, do it. Just watch how many men will flaunt to your side.

Now, I know it's very easy for me to tell you to control your emotions, because I can. That's like you telling me to start showing my emotions more…I can't because it's not in my DNA. But I can be aware of it and control it to some extent.

If you have a broken heart, the pain is going to be there and your emotions are going to have you screaming and crying. I know. I just want you to understand the power you can wield if you choose to not let your emotions take over your actions.

You basically neuter a man because that's all he has over you. And when you realize this power "take away", you and your emotions will want to step away from the situation.

Start acting like a guy would and watch the pendulum swing…IT'S AMAZING!

 **#7: Man Mode**

Ok, Man Mode. This is the state of mind that is my secret sauce to getting what you want from men. We are going to get deep here, so hang on and bear with me.

"Gregg, is this is a game?"

Fuck yeah, it's a game. Relationships are a game. Love is a game. Life is a game. I'm tired of people thinking that love should be a fairy tale and end like a Cinderella story where all is well. That's a wonderful thought but I wouldn't be selling 100 books a day if this were true. Love takes work! AND a few little games.

If two people are in love, they can control their own fate and longevity by knowing HOW to COMMUNICATE.

55% of the time marriage ends in divorce. And of the other 45% that stay together, I say there is another 10% that simply cohabitate because of kids. And another 10% are just friends that sleep in separate beds down the hall.

So by my math (granted, this is not scientific but I believe it to be true) that leaves 25% that MIGHT make it… and I even think that is high!

Play love my way and by my rules and watch your odds triple! If it makes you feel better, let's not call it a GAME. Let's call it an "occasional rule change" or "let's put an extra player on the ice" for you at times.

Or let's just call it MAN MODE.

Plain and simple: Man Mode is a state of mind that wom-

en need to put themselves into, on occasion, to get what they want from a man and to keep the relationship thriving by communicating in a way that HE understands.

Yes, I made up this term and it sounds stupid but we can re-name it something cooler later…whatever.

This state of mind that YOU are going to learn is very similar to how a man talks to his male friends. It can also be compared to the relationship women have with gay men. Defenses are taken down in both of these scenarios. And when defenses are down, communication can REALLY happen.

I mean, doesn't it blow your mind how easily a guy can talk to a guy? It's almost like we are in love. Actually, we are but without the sex. Think about it, guys touch, they spend tons of time together, and they spill their emotions on each other. They show their soft underbellies. These are ALL the things YOU want but instead a "wall" gets put up because YOU represent a threat to his manhood.

I mean a tough, bad-ass guy who rides a Harley can be emotional with his buddies before his girlfriend…what gives?

Men think like this:

- You will take our friends away from us.

- You will force us to have sex with ONLY you.

- You will take our money.

Sounds sad, huh? The funny thing is we **want** you to take some of our friends away. We **want** to just have sex with one awesome girl—you. And we **want** to provide and spend our money on you.

But we're stupid and we need YOU to show us the way! Otherwise, our shallow extended college lives will remain intact.

If you communicate with a man and keep his masculinity in check, you will become his prize AND get what YOU WANT!

Many women are very jealous of this guy/guy relationship and they don't know how to deal with it. So they react the way they know best—they get emotional. Statements like "Why do you always want to spend more time with your friends than with me?" come out. And this is poison to the relationship.

What if you could be that girlfriend/wife/lover AND have that same capability to get him to DROP his defenses just like he does with his close male friends?

Hmmm? Go on.

This would be done without him even knowing what is going on. Man Mode is just a slight shift in your persona. That's all it is. Basically, I'm just going to get you to re-direct your emotional energy into an energy that a man understands through a series of everyday occurrences. Just a like the man-man relationship.

Sounds simple, right? It is!

I am talking about relationships right now but this applies across the board. Once you understand and can execute Man Mode, you can use it when you are totally single to attract guys too. I'll get into all of that later. For now, let's stick with our relationship examples and assume you are dating a guy/have a boyfriend or are married. And this guy is starting to go rogue.

Rogue is defined as when a guy starts taking you for granted. You are starting to lose him. This is explained in detail in my book: *Who Holds the Cards Now?*

Ok ,Gregg, how do I execute Man Mode?

Man Mode starts with a list of things that you are going to do AND, just as importantly, a list of things that CANNOT happen in the relationship scenario we have placed you in. Remember, this tactic ONLY gets used on occasion.

Three things to remember:

- *When in doubt, treat a man like a man and CONFRONT him*

- *"Catch me if you can" should be your new motto*

- *Take the emotion away when dealing with him*

Back to the main threats that women represent:

- **You will take our friends away from us**

- **You will force us to have sex with ONLY you**

- **You will take our money**

This is your NEW way to deal with these three threats:

<u>*You will take our friends away.*</u> Don't take our friends away—let us take OURSELVES away from our friends. We want to, but give us reason by making yourself so

attractive and interesting that we would rather be with you. In fact, encourage us to be with our friends. Then go be with yours. We will be left thinking, hmm, I want to spend more time with her.

The chapter about "making yourself interesting" (coming next) comes into play here. If you have passions to pursue, you become attractive to us. Suddenly, nachos and Xbox seem a little immature and we call you.

Of course, the irony is that many women that follow my advice LEAVE the Xbox man eating nachos and start dating a quality man they meet through their interests!!!

Maybe this is why I am writing books for women, because of all the death threats I get…Hmmm.

You will force us to have sex with only you. Again, don't tell us that you want to be exclusive—make us want to be exclusive with you. Lead us there. Mature quality men don't need more "notches on their belt." They want a woman to fall in love with. By bringing confidence, you become a woman of value to us. Having your own goals in life and taking time away from us to pursue them, makes you attractive to us.

We realize that we are not your hobby and that your time is valuable. This, in turn, makes us try harder. Then other women can't compare and all our resources and drive are concentrated on you.

You will take our money. Don't ask us to buy you things—make us WANT to provide for you and we will buy you things. Do this by paying your way or at least always offering. Men are extremely cognizant of gold diggers and when you prove that you want us for our personality, we give up our money willingly.

More Man Mode points to know:

Arguing. When you start to argue, you are going to say less and withdraw just like he does, but YOU are going to do it first. Maybe you leave the house and go meet your friends. But don't show anger.

Texting. You are going to text like you tweet. One short sentence and to the point. No emotion and always let him text last. Just like a man.

I have the #1 texting book in the world and I advise you to get it: *Power Texting Men.*

Sex. If you are having sex, try to role reverse this too. Be aggressive. Don't communicate afterwards and maybe go home or go to sleep. If you are always pushing for an orgasm, forget about it. Get him off and leave it at that. Remember, we are talking on occasion here and when a man goes rogue.

Don't bitch and whine. Guys don't react to this. We stop communicating and we withdraw. Don't suppress your emotions, no. Take them to your girlfriends. Think guy here. Our guy friends don't bitch and whine. They confront or withdraw…do the same once in a while.

Tell him like it is. This is how guys communicate. If a guy has bad breath, his friend says, "Dude your breath smells like shit. Chew some gum will you." This is innate to men.

We don't sugarcoat anything, so contempt can never build and the problem is FIXED. Women, on the other hand, talk behind each other's backs so nothing gets solved.

Basically, you are going to change right in front of him and ACT like his best guy friend. This is similar to what I explain in *Who Holds the Cards Now?*. He will smile and laugh and be perplexed. This is good. This is acceptance and will get him to drop his defenses just like he does with his guy friends. Do this enough and he starts to associate you as a non-threatening friend as well as his lover.

And the beauty is, the more emotional you have been in the past, the better Man Mode works. IF you can pull it off—CUT OUT THE EMOTION.

You will find your guy will start to take more interest in you. You have become interesting and mysterious to him again, just like the early days. You are communicating to him in a way he understands now. No longer does he get scolded for his actions. Instead, you confront him and just walk out the door. And he is left standing alone and WANTING to communicate. Wow!

Then, when the power starts to "shift", you go into "catch me if you can mode." If he gets horny, you say, "Not tonight. Heading out with my friends. Maybe tomorrow."

Now it's important to remember that Man Mode only has to happen on occasion. And it doesn't have to happen only when your needs aren't getting met. Just SHOW him that you have it in you. Of course, he doesn't even know what is happening in real life.

He walks in the room with a crappy shirt on and you say with a smile, "Where did you get that shirt? The Salvation Army?", when you would normally let him wear it and keep it to yourself (or tell your girlfriend).

The smile is important. Otherwise, you are just being mean. This is what guys do and it works. Now, he might not change his shirt—that's not important—but he respects this confrontation from you. You are standing up to him, which represents POWER, BOUNDARIES and RESPECT—just like his male friends.

Guys CONFRONT each other. This is how they communicate and build respect with each other. You need to do the same.

Confront your man at times. Not with anger, but with point-blank accuracy on what he is doing wrong. Tell him exactly what you feel without getting all lovey, pissed off or emotional about it. Don't change who you are—just have this confrontational quality in you. When in doubt, do it just like his friends do.

Let's use me as an example:

My girlfriend confronts me sometimes and she gets away with it. Why? Because I get out of line on occasion. ALL men do. Men like to test people. This is our competitive nature. Other times we are just stupid and overlook you.

I used to get out of the car and walk ten steps ahead of her. (This is one of my bad quirks.) She didn't put up with it and she didn't get upset. Instead, she cupped her hands together and yelled, "Hey boyfriend, do you want to walk with me or should I find a guy that will?"

Perfect! She just treated me like a guy and I listened. She smiled through the whole thing and I was NEVER scolded. There was NO residual anger or anything…just like a guy…EASY and MAGICAL.

And guess what? It didn't happen again because she communicated in a way that I understood and will remember. This is Man Mode.

She called me on it and I got back in line. She doesn't wear the boots, no, but she CAN when she needs to and THAT'S the difference.

And when she decides to wear the boots?

SHE RULES ME!

God, I hate to admit that.

Other women I have dated have tried to wear the boots and would TELL me all the time "how it's going to be." In the example above I would get yelled at, for real, and she would be angry throughout the night. She would bring it up in the future too.

She would last about a day with me.

This is NOT Man Mode.

Other women would set no boundaries and let me do whatever I wanted to just to keep me "happy." In the example above, a woman would just let me walk 10 paces in front of her. I would (finally) realize it after a while and wonder why she didn't say anything. She would be the type to let me get away with anything and she would probably make me her hobby.

She would last about a week.

Are you getting my point here?

Yes, I know, guys are assholes!

No.

Man Mode is a balance. You're like an inside domestic cat that is pleasant to be around and who cuddles and purrs. Then you get let outside (your man goes rogue) and all hell breaks loose.

You don't get mad. This is important. Think about how a guy treats a guy. You make the statement and get over it! Two guys give each other crap and in the next minute all is forgotten and the problem is solved.

Never, NEVER say something like "we need to talk." This instantly triggers our defensive mode and you will NOT solve your problem. Contempt will build. Again, think like a guy. No guy ever tells his buddy, "We need to talk."

Well, maybe as a joke to make fun of women. :)

#8: Make Yourself an Interesting Person

If you want a guy to take interest in you, then become an interesting person.

Sounds simple, right? But many women aren't doing this! They contact me because they are losing their man, or have lost their man, and they don't have a clue why. They tell me how beautiful they are and strong, etc. But they aren't interesting to their guy because they have NO interests!

I don't know about you, but I'm attracted to INTER-ESTING people. Why? Because I find them fascinating to listen to and I can learn something new in life or add to the conversation with my own experience on the subject, if I have any. Interesting women can sexually and emotionally attract a man. And this is the PROPER way to do it. Quality men are thinking long term. If you are boring and have no interests, then we know that we will be bored in a matter of weeks with you.

Now, I know one's personality can go a long way towards making a person interesting and exciting. But we are talking long term here. If two people keep their interests evolving both together and separate, they will always be interesting because they will fill their respective "jars" with exciting experiences.

If you attract us with your cleavage hanging out, we will just want SEX from you. But if you attract us with your mind, knowledge and experiences—we will want ALL of you.

What do I see out there? I see boring-ass men and women who can only expand on the latest reality shows. WTF?

My world revolves around meeting people and interviewing them, whether they know it or not. I pay particular attention to gorgeous women and older couples. Let's talk about gorgeous women.

Last week I grabbed a beer at The SandBar in Delray Beach, FL. I was talking to this hot twenty-five-year-old girl. I could barely keep her to myself with all the men trying their best to "cock block" me. She was very attractive.

This woman was smart but she had NOTHING going on in her life. She went on and on about her failed relationships. I asked her why she didn't have any real interests or hobbies and she said she doesn't need any because the men in her life exposed her to THEIR hobbies.

Needless to say, I told her what I do and you can bet the men around us, in her eyes, magically disappeared. I told her (respectably) what was missing in her life and I think I changed her thinking in a BIG way.

My point here is not to bloviate my skills, but to show you that even a gorgeous, smart woman won't survive without "being interesting." These men want to slam her and, when that gets old, they'll move on.

Now take "average" looking women that DO have interests. Same trip, I'm at The SandBar and I met a group of surfers. These ladies were very average looking but they were INTERESTING. I mean, when I got on their subject, their personalities BLOSSOMED.

These women were SO much more interesting to me (and the group of guys I was with) than the hot one will ever be. Yes, looks initially attract us, but that fades and guys know it. WE want to settle down with a woman with interests and THAT is the way to attract us.

To attract and keep a man, YOU need to be an interesting person. This means you need EXPERIENCES. The more experiences you have, the better. If you travel, sky-dive, can make balloon animals, dance, kickbox or raise awareness for stray dogs, then YOU have something interesting to talk about, teach or share.

Never stop. NEVER, NEVER stop. Couples are notorious for this. They join at the hip but stop growing. Excuses like kids or work come into play. They stagnate. They become boring to each other. Then they stray apart and—SNAP…it's over.

If you are single, pay SPECIAL attention to this chapter. REJOICE that you are single. This is the EASIEST and BEST time to grow and take on new experiences. And guess what? An extraordinary guy is going to show his face and you will have found him, where? Nope, not at a club. Yes, you guessed it, pursuing a new hobby or experience.

This chapter is HUGE. If you followed through on this one point –

Experience as many things as you can so you can bring an arsenal of value to a potential lover.

You will have a flood of men knocking down your door. Trust me.

#9: Baggage Handling

Unlike the airport, we are going to handle your baggage properly.

Let's talk about women's (and men's) baggage that may affect a relationship and how to deal with it from a guy's perspective.

Kids, health issues, depression, financial woes, an angry stalker or maybe a total lack of trust are all common examples of the baggage we bring.

First off, we ALL have baggage, even when we think we don't. Sometimes no baggage is even baggage. Let's take me again as an example. I'm getting into my late forties and I don't have kids. What? What is wrong with you?

Exactly.

Women sometimes look at me and ask why I don't have kids. Ironically, they would feel better if I had three and I was divorced! That's how ugly this world stands when it comes to relationships. People want to date failures!

This becomes my baggage. Men react very differently than women when it comes to baggage and it's important for you to grasp where we stand.

By the way, in case you forgot, I have thousands of guys each week visit my website and talk all about dating women, so the words I speak are from a huge sampling of men and not just MY opinion.

Here are my three ways to expose YOUR baggage properly:

Get it out there. If we find out you have kids on the second date, we will feel duped. Maybe not because you have kids BUT because you left that out. We will think, "What else did you leave out?" Now, this doesn't mean it needs to be the first sentence out of your mouth, but we want this information available to us early so we can decide if this is ok or not.

Remember, every man has some baggage. And ours is sitting there too. We are actually relieved when a woman comes out and is honest with us.

Keep it light and tell us you are working on it. If you have some bad baggage, frame it to us in a light way. If you have trust issues say, "I'm doing my best to trust men, but it's been a hard road." This is good. This tells us you are working on trusting more. Other women will say, "I've been screwed over so many times in the past with guys, I can't trust anymore."

Ok, tell me where the exit is.

If it's minor, leave it be. We are tough and we have dealt with some really bad examples of women. Stalkers, coke heads and out right crazy women have crossed most guys paths if they've dated into their thirties. Don't sweat it.

Now, if you have major emotional issues, you should NOT be dating. These need to be dealt with professionally. A man is NOT the answer.

Ok, Gregg, how do I find out about a GUY'S baggage?

I thought you would never ask. First off, DON'T ask him, because he probably won't tell you.

Yes, I know, we can suck and I'm not always proud of what I teach in my books but it's the truth. You wouldn't want it any other way.

You can ask him if he has kids. Kids may or may not be baggage to you. You can ask him about his job. If he doesn't have a job, then THIS is baggage. If he has a crappy job, then this could be baggage. But when you ask him about drugs, alcohol or herpes, it begins to sound more like an interview and we may get defensive even though these are legitimate concerns.

If you start to get serious with any man, do a criminal record check on him. It's easy, inexpensive and could save you a world of trouble. Trust is earned, and he hasn't earned anything from you yet.

The way to find out a man's baggage is to take him out on dates that will expose EVERYTHING about him. He will have no choice.

Watch how he treats people. Does he tip well? Does he open doors and practice chivalry? Does he drink too much? Does he drive drunk? Does he mention or do drugs? Does he get jealous? Does he get mad easily? Is he a complainer? Is he a tightwad with his money? Is he a slob, overspender or just plain lazy?

You see, now YOU are a woman of value and you are the chooser. LOOK for these things. In the past maybe you just saw that awesome body or those baby blue eyes.

Now you know what you must have in a man and what you can and cannot compromise on. AND you have an abundance of men because you have interests and you have met various quality men through these interests.

This is your NEW playbook and WOW what a difference it will make.

Here are my four ways to get HIS baggage exposed early:

Meet his friends. Another super way of discovering a guy's baggage is by meeting his friends. This is when you will see where he stands among his peers and if they have respect for him and how. If all his friends are players, then guess what? He is too. If he sides with his friends instead of you, hit the exits—immediately. Maybe he hit you with a ton of lies and now his friends are accidentally revealing them.

Again, hit the exit.

Meet his family. Obviously, this will not happen until a bit later but maybe you can "accidentally" run into them. Here you will see how he acts around his Mom…very telling! If he is a Mama's boy, I would be careful. If he doesn't respect her, then be very careful. If she doesn't respect him, he will have some major issues too. Family rarely lies. And Moms are notorious for putting junior in an uncomfortable position.

My Mom always mentions how my three older sisters would dress me up in girls' clothing. Embarrassing? Yes, but I can live with it.

But if you get, "Jimmy has always had a drinking problem, which he got from his alcoholic father, but I'm sure you can clean him up."

Exit.

Have your friends meet him. Your close friends will be able to see things that you will not always be able to. Maybe he is checking out other women when you look away or even hitting on your friends! Maybe he picks his nose every time he looks away, who knows? Yes, your friends will help you and it can be very telling information. They can also be the "bad guys" and hit him with the tough questions that you should avoid at this early stage:

> *"Hey Jeff, so what's your deal, why have you never been married? Are you a player?"*

I tell women to formulate a plan with specific questions to "interview" your date. You can always say to him later, "Don't listen to Kim. She's a bit protective of me."

Get him drunk. I catch shit for this one but it works! Alcohol is like a man's truth serum. USE IT! The key here is that YOU need to stay sober. Join him when he is drunk with his friends already. If he is drunk alone, not good. What is he like? Does he want to fight everyone? Does he want to have sex with you and announce it to the world? Does he jump into a dumpster like some idiot?

Oh, the knowledge that can be gained by a twelve-pack and 3 shots of Cuervo is precious!

You want to see a man that is cool when he has had a

few too many. Ideally, you want a man that rarely has a few too many. He should be responsible, respectable and show no "demons."

Covertly. Ok, I won't count this as one because I never mentioned it. :) You know what I mean. Looking through a guy's medicine cabinet and peeking here and there are ALL things women do and I don't blame you.

Guys are usually bad about hiding stuff from women—we don't cover our tracks well. We leave our cell phones hanging around and we think our bathrooms are for taking a piss and blowing farts. Car storage compartments?—Viagra and lube for potential car sex. Computer history?—Porn sites.

You get my point.

In essence, these areas are a plethora of information.

If you see athletes foot medication in the drawer—no big deal. But when multiple cases of condoms and a Japanese swing appear in his apartment? Run.

Remember, this paragraph was not written by me.

Follow these steps above and your baggage will smell sweet. His baggage will be strewn out all over the place for you to see and to decide if this is your future or not!

#10: My Formula for Attraction

Get Busy = Build Confidence = Lure Quality Men

Nothing attracts a man more than a woman who is busy. First, let's define a busy woman. A busy woman is:

- In college and pursuing a REAL career

- Advancing in a career

- Involved with a hobby or many hobbies

- Really GOOD at something after years of training

- A girl who has little time in her day due to her activities

I'm not talking about a girl who is busy shopping or busy doing cocaine with all her friends. I'm not talking about a woman that can FB all day and kick ass at video games.

A busy woman has interests and this makes her an interesting person. She then can teach her interests to others or mesh with others doing her same gig. This builds confidence and fills up her jar with experiences that she can share with the world.

Her time is valuable. Why would she waste her time on some useless couch vegetable when she can go surfing with her buds? She chooses men. And they are from the top of the apple tree and not rotting on the ground.

She has boundaries and she sets them. Sex is given out

on a "worthy" basis and that's not often. Phone numbers don't go to strangers and the bar scene is a joke to these busy, high value women.

Men see busy women as a challenge. They want what they can't have and these women are THEIR upper fruit. These women are not needy or in any rush to have kids and guys know this. They know this girl will never be needy or clingy and they love this.

Men will bring their A game to court these women because they represent a massive challenge.

I always bring up the domestic cat/human relationship. When you want your cat Gizmo to come to you, what does he do? He heads in the other direction. So you start to give chase to the cute, furry beast. Where does he go? Under the bed where you can't get him.

Now try ignoring Gizmo because you're busy. What does he do? He's confused, he's lonely. He sees you as a busy confident woman and wants to be on your lap all the time purring with pleasure. :)

I am actually talking about my own cat (Gizmo) who is on my lap right now as I write. :)

Men are like Gizmo. Just worse. If you pursue a man he naturally runs. No challenge and no sense of mystery. But when you are a busy woman, things change. He thinks, "She has no time for me so I gotta try harder—I WANT her!"

Again, it's amazingly simple and yet how often is a woman REALLY busy working on her life? My answer, at least from the women that contact me, is NOT often. I find ladies to be just the opposite of busy. They are busy alright, pursuing any breathing, high baggage man that will give her some attention.

No! No! and No! This is what society teaches us. *Get a man and be happy.* They missed one thing:

Get a life, *then get a man and be happy!*

The *life part* is the confident part. And the confident part is what lures the men like a cat to tuna. If every woman did this, their issues would be solved and I would be out of business. But as a society we are taught to be in a big rush. We are told to start a family, in my opinion, much too early.

Let's change this. It's never too late.

Get Busy = Build Confidence = Lure Quality Men

You need to become a busy, confident woman. So stop making guys your key to happiness and start getting BUSY!

Then, watch the men bulldoze to your front door! Build her and they will come.

#11: Physical Improvement

"Our growing softness,
our increasing lack of physical activity,
is a menace to our security."
—John F. Kennedy

I'm sorry but this chapter needs to be in this book. I happen to be a Beachbody coach so I have seen many girls' and guys' transformations, as well as my own. And not just in our bodies—in our CONFIDENCE!

The power of working out and eating healthy cannot be discounted!

We are talking confidence in this book and where and how to get it, right? I know that very few people enjoy the process of getting in shape, but the results cannot be denied. Hell, I can't stand working out! But after the workout? I'm telling you, I'm in a state of bliss. You know the feeling. You did yoga for an hour or you rode the bike and did some weights—when you're done, you feel GREAT! These are your endorphins screaming with pleasure!

So let's use this to kickstart our new lives. Let's use working out as our first step to greatness and becoming a higher value person. Let's use physical improvement to keep us busy, be our first new hobby and potentially create new social circles!

Whether we're talking about an entire nation or an individual, the above quote is true. Your physical conditioning directly correlates to your level of security or confidence. This is a sore subject for many girls, no pun intended. It's no secret that the physical appearance of a person helps determine their level of attractiveness. Yet somehow this obvious reality is often swept aside. Part of the reason is that there are women in great physical shape who are horrible at getting men. And likewise, there are overweight girls who manage to meet quality men effortlessly.

So if your fitness is so important, how can this possibly be? The answer is simple. Fit women who lack the confidence and skills to effectively sell themselves to men will fail nonetheless. And out of shape girls who have a strong sense of confidence and self-esteem, and who have a good grasp on what they want in a man and what makes men tick, will often manage to overcome their physical flaws.

None of this matters to you though, because if you're reading this you need help in one of the two areas. Either you happen to be in good shape and need help meeting men or you're in bad shape and you need help meeting men. I guess, in a sense, if you're already physically fit you have a bit of a leg up going into this course. That's good because you need all the help you can get on your journey to success.

If you're like most women, however, especially if you're a bit older, you're not in very good shape. And that's normal and okay. For many of us, we weren't taught proper body maintenance growing up. Or maybe we were naturally healthy when we were younger but didn't have the skills to combat Father Time. Perhaps others were fit before, like in high school, but let themselves go.

The road to weight problems is fraught with excuses. No time. No money. No need. Wrong. Wrong. Wrong. We already covered the last one and we know you need this. The time excuse is particularly bogus. You don't need to spend hours in the gym every day to see dramatic results. As you travel on the path to physical wellness, that may be a choice you decide to make because it simply feels so good to workout at a high level. But you're nowhere near that right now anyway. It's not even advisable to start off pushing too hard.

It is perfectly sufficient to spend a half hour a day, five days a week, walking or jogging. And then add in two to three days a week doing some sort of resistance workout as you'd do at the gym. We're talking about maybe five hours a week, if that. The not-surprising fact is that by improving your physical strength and conditioning, you are more effective in life and you bring more confidence. You have more energy, you work better, you play better, and you feel better. This releases time back in your favor. If it takes you less time to do things in life, and if you're enjoying your life more as well, then you actually *gain* time in the equation.

The money excuse is just as insidious. A membership to the gym is maybe thirty dollars a month on average. That's about seven dollars a week. Now factor in the foods you eat and how much. By improving your diet, which we'll discuss in a bit, and by eating less food, you'll be able to easily make up for the gym membership many times over. In fact, you'll have plenty of extra funds just by changing how you eat, to help finance new hairstyles, makeup and, of course, new clothes.

I'm sure you're coming up with some other excuses already, so I need to address something very important. In order to improve yourself physically, you need to become a master of focus and determination. In other words, what's been holding you back is mostly mental. This starts with first accepting your age and your present condition. It's okay. You're not eighteen anymore. Start where you are and work from there. Stop defeating yourself out of the gate. Just as with the other areas of this book, you need to take small, gradual steps.

And if you are eighteen, it's just as important. You see working out is NOT just about looking good to the other sex. It's psychological. When you work out, you are busy and you are feeling good about yourself. Endorphins are being released! Simply put, there is no better way to start gaining your confidence back then by starting to get in shape.

Commit yourself to consistency. This isn't the same as perfection. Understand that in order to accomplish physical improvement, it's much more important to chip away in small increments on a regular basis than it is to pack in power workouts. This will also help prevent injuries and keep you in the game. Start small and add intensity one week at a time. Create a fitness-friendly environment and eliminate as much stress from your life as possible. Also make sure to get a good night's sleep every night so your body and mind can rest and recover.

Pick an activity, or group of activities, you like doing that involves thirty minutes of cardio. This can be as simple as walking or hiking a nearby trail. In fact, walking is one of the best low-impact activities you can do. It's also been scientifically proven that a brisk walk is as close to our experience as an infant walking on all fours as we can get. This is important because walking naturally aligns yourself to your Self. It's a great way to remind your body who and what you are. If you add in a natural environment, like a mountain hike or a local park, you're also communing with nature and that's good for your mind, body and soul.

Yes, there is a spiritual side to working out with nature that will help you too, whether you believe in this or not. Try it.

Other activities might include swimming, biking, playing sports, or anything that gets your heart racing for a consistent period of time. And DON'T overdo it. This will not only expose you to injuries that could hamper your goals but it also has the effect of discouraging you because you feel like the next workout is going to be too much.

Now hit the gym. The big advantage of the gym is all the equipment and the ability to pack in a full body workout in a short period of time. Most memberships include a free evaluation with a trainer, so take advantage of that. They will help you set a program to paper so you can focus and track your results. Also, look to online resources, books, magazines, anything to improve your knowledge on training.

Personally, I like doing P90X, Insanity and T25 workouts. I respond well to someone yelling at me on a video. And, shit, if you are going to get in shape, why not go all in? That's up to you, but it works for me and tens of thousands of others.

Either way, make sure and develop a complete strength regimen that includes all the basic muscle groups. Work on your biceps, triceps, chest and back. And pay special attention to your abs. Not only is this immensely sexy to the men (a tight stomach), but your core is where your central energy emits from. By strengthening your core, you are toning your entire body. And don't worry, ladies, you will not grow big muscles. Just keep the weight light and the reps high…and stay off the steroids. :)

As you begin burning calories and building lean muscle, it is vital to pay attention to and alter your food intake as well. And first off, much of what you're likely consuming isn't even classified as food. Ditch *all* liquid calories right away. The sodas, the sugar in your coffee, anything that's not directly nourishing your body needs to go. These are empty calories. Beer is too, girls, so keep an eye on it.

Substitute in lots of vegetables, some fruits and whole grains. You want to be eating real food. Food that is supplying your body with what it needs to be healthy. The great thing about vegetables is the variety and the fact that they have almost zero calories. You can prepare them in an infinite number of ways and combine them with all types of dishes. The vitamins and minerals they release also help improve your mental functioning and the overall chemistry of your body, and that allows you to get fitter faster.

When we're talking about vegetables, it's all about color. You want to include all the different colors available. If you look at your salad or stir-fry and it looks like an artist's palette, then you're on the right track.

You want to eat fruits more sparingly. While they are good for you, and completely necessary, they are also high in sugar. To help balance this out, try and combine fruits with a healthy fatty food, like a slice of cheese or some nuts. The reason why is that fats burn the slowest in your body, while sugars and carbs burn the fastest, so they help balance each other out. Proteins land somewhere in between. This is why you want to build around a balanced diet of lean proteins, healthy fats and simple carbs. This creates the alchemy of change your body is craving.

Luckily, there is a vast amount of literature on the subject. Make yourself an expert. And avoid fad diets or obscure recommendations. All you really have to do is exercise, eat a healthy balanced diet and you'll see amazing results. You don't need the latest workout machine or some restricted diet. Use common sense.

Once you've got your exercise and food situation on track, focus on other elements of your physical appearance. Make sure you find a hair stylist you like. Again, you don't need to spend a ton of money, but, like clothes, it is worth investing enough to get quality as this will pay off in spades. Find someone you're comfortable with who you can afford and stick with them. I've found that over time working with the same stylist pays dividends, as they get to know you and your hair and can help evolve you over time to help make you look better.

And remember your smile, or lack of one, has an affect too. Studies show that girls who don't smile much tend to hook up with men for short-term matches, while smiling girls attract long-term relationships. This obviously isn't a black or white thing, but be aware of the impressions and facial expressions you're giving off.

Your body is truly your temple. It's your sanctuary. And in a very real sense it helps provide your inner security and confidence. When you're in shape, you're ready to handle life on a higher level. You feel better about yourself mentally, and you just feel better, period. Take care of your body and it will take care of you. And there is simply no excuse for not looking good.

So let's use this to kickstart our new lives. Let's use working out as our first step to greatness and becoming a higher value person. Let's use physical improvement to keep us busy, be our first new hobby and potentially create new social circles!

OVERVIEW

- Physical health is a mindset you have to want

- Excuses are unacceptable

- Join a gym

- Commit yourself to consistency

- Slow and steady wins the race

- List activities you enjoy doing and do them

- Do cardio five days a week for 30 minutes

- Do strength conditioning at least twice a week

- Do some yoga

- Lower calories and eliminate liquid calories

- Revamp your diet to whole foods only

- Eat lots of vegetables and a little fruit too

- Keep educating yourself on proper eating habits

- Concentrate on your smile too :)

#12: Shock Some Confidence into Yourself

"Do one thing every day that scares you."
—Eleanor Roosevelt

My Secret Tip

Sometimes we have to put the self-help books down, shut off Doctor Phil and solve our problems like a MAN. Or, in this case, like a WOMAN.

I want to throw this out at you and see if I can get you to take the challenge! My true life example is a guy, but this applies to women too.

My friend Artie is the perfect example. Artie participates in girl-perusing antics quite often. He makes great money and is an above-average looking man. He listens to me and he practices what I preach in my male books. But he is still having a tough time. His confidence is like a roller coaster. He allows external forces to influence him. For example, he feels great when we go out and he gets a number or engages with women, but lousy when he gets rejected.

I felt Artie needed something different than a book.

Some people can't, or they just don't, respond to affirmations and goal-setting. A self-help book simply won't help them. Maybe it's just a lack of concentration or ADD, but my close friend Artie was not where he wanted to be, both in his personal life and with women.

I found this frustrating. If I couldn't help a close friend gain confidence, then how could I justify helping others?

For my own good, I needed to fix him.

Some people will not respond to mental exercises or self-help books. They need an outside force to change. This change can be an activity that is outside their comfort zone.

Artie is conservative guy. I find this a common trait among people with low self-esteem. He does not take chances. His day is very organized and scripted. His weekends don't get much better. I wanted Artie to take a risk…a huge risk! I wanted him to get TOTALLY outside of his comfort zone. I had a plan that did not involve any mental exercises.

I set up a day of skydiving. I knew he would never go so I had to lie to him about my plan. He thought we were going to Six Flags Amusement Park. When he realized he was being redirected, things got a bit hairy. I really gave him no choice, and kudos to him for not backing out. This was only accomplished by telling him how much this was costing me and that this was a 2-day deal. Day 1 we train, day 2 we jump. Artie felt he had a way out.

He didn't.

Day 1 we train and jump!

Amazingly, the influence and confidence of our instructors, and the fact that they'd been in this position before with hesitant guys and girls that did NOT want to jump, somehow convinced Artie that he was not going to die. Combine this with the fact that he would have to live with the reality that he wimped out on me, put his back against the wall.

He jumped!

Truth be told, I almost shit a brick myself. I am afraid of heights, but because my friend was worse off, I could deal with it better.

The result: truly AMAZING!

This jump changed his mindset. He started to challenge himself. If I had a parachute for every time he said, "Shit, I fucking jumped out of a plane, I sure as hell can do (fill in the blank)", well, I would have a lot of parachutes!

Artie took a risk that day. One could argue he took the biggest risk of his life. He stepped out of his comfort zone. Granted I had to lie to him and manipulate the poor bastard, but it worked.

On a side note, I helped myself. I stepped out of **my** comfort zone too. I felt more invigorated towards life and "charged up" for days going forward. I also helped a friend and this increased my commitment to being a "man of value."

Now, I can't say this one challenge gave Artie all the confidence he ever needed. He still has his days of very low self-esteem…we all do. But short of a near death experience, Artie has made vast improvements. His days are no longer mundane. He is much more socially aggressive.

Of course, skydiving is my extreme example. Find yours. I want it to be 5 times more extreme than your personality would allow. The activity should stir some fear and some emotion. Think dangerous fun.

1) Bungee jump

2) Hit a rollercoaster

3) Race in a Winston Cup car (I did this in Las Vegas, tons of fun!)

4) Surf, jet ski, sail

5) Rock climb, hike a mountain

6) Ride in a fighter jet

7) Dog sled ride, skidoo

8) Jump in the ocean in the winter

9) Anything that is outside your comfort zone

*Step out of your zone, take a risk
and feel the euphoria of confidence.*

I think we all should skydive. It's scary and there is the possibility of dying (at least in our minds) and the human brain reacts positively to this. I never wish a near-death experience on anyone, but I feel those that have had one are BETTER for it. People can gain confidence by realizing how precious and short life can be. Just talk to someone who's survived cancer or a car crash. What happens? They start LIVING. They say, "I cheated death so I am going to live today like it is my last!"

Living life with this fresh perspective will allow you to experience more things that you would never do. With more experiences comes more learning, growing and confidence.

My advice to you is: "Do one thing every day that scares you," and watch how self-esteem pours into your mind and body.

The BEST way to your build confidence is to fire up your endorphins and use that adrenaline!

#13: Maybe He is Just an Asshole: Dump his Ass!

Sometimes we just get ourselves into bad relationships. It happens. Some guys simply suck. They don't know what they want, they don't know how to communicate, they can't get out of their college years, they have no self-esteem, they're liars, cheaters or they go MIA for no reason at all.

Women often blame themselves for the behavior of these assholes and may even lower themselves to pathetic levels just to try to keep the relationship alive.

And what does this toxic relationship end up doing to you? It wastes precious weeks, months and even years of your time, beats up your self-esteem, causes you major pain, and makes you bitter for the rest of your life.

This book is about understanding men so you can recognize these assholes and take your power back. In this chapter I want to point out some of the different types of assholes (many of which you probably know very well) and make sure you avoid them. Remember, you are STRONG now so you don't need these losers.

So my wonderful readers, I want to introduce a new way of thinking: _If a guy doesn't treat you the way you want to be treated, it's time to blame him and not you._

He might just be an asshole.

I have been teaching you to become a woman of value, raise your expectations and set boundaries.

And when you do this, you approach dating from a position of power and not from a place of weakness.

Amazing things happen, including, attracting ONLY quality confident men.

Use Your Intuition

As you build up your self-esteem, your best friend will be back to join you. Do you remember her? Her name is Intuition. She has always been there for you but you didn't always trust her in the past.

TRUST YOUR BEST FRIEND!

I'm a guy and I have some degree of intuition. But you? My God, girl, I can't believe how accurate and how honed your intuition can be. I speak from experience. You see, I was that asshole through my twenties (regrettably.) And I was always amazed how women were smack on correct with me when I wasn't being "up front" with them.

I mean, I could usually convince them that I did love them and that I was going to call them. The reality was I didn't love them and I wasn't going to call them. They were correct—I was an asshole—but they didn't trust their intuition.

You, on the other hand, can trust your intuition again. So you will never settle on a man that doesn't deliver on the basics. This is ONLY the starting point of a good man.

Make Sure He Delivers on the Basics!

Here are some of the basics:

Basic 101: Prompt contact—He goes MIA.

Assholes do this all the time. They go incognito because they're lazy and they're assholes. If a guy can't give you the decency of a prompt call back or text, then lose his ass. I mean, come on, really? Your best friend (Miss Intuition) knows that he is lazy, selfish and is not into you. This also applies to the early stages of the relationship where days may go by without contact as he tells you he is out-of-town or something.

A text takes five seconds and can happen from all over the world—NO EXCUSE.

Now you can politely present the issue to this man and say, "Yo boyfriend, what's up with the disappearing act? The guy for me needs to respond a little more or I will find someone else who will." You are strong and there is nothing wrong with having this conversation. If he continues?

He is the problem not you—He is an asshole—Dump his ass.

Basic 102: He's got a decent job or is well on his way.

Come on, girls, do you really want a man who you need to pay for all the time? A guy that needs to mooch off his friends all the time or is still living with his parents at age 30? Where will this relationship really go? I don't care about the hot sex, lizard tongue or chiseled chin.

Remember the conveyer belt of manhood? A guy needs a sense of self-worth and that is defined by who he is, what he does and if he can provide. Yes, that means he needs money. If he doesn't have it, then he cannot love because he won't love himself. He is a wet kitten because he has no career.

And when Daddy gives him his inheritance, everything will be good, right? Nope, he will dump your ass,
never pay you back and upgrade to some pole dancer
bitch who used to be a man.

I digress.

He doesn't need to be rich. He just needs a sound career that he is happy with. I will let you determine the
importance of how much money he needs to get paid
for you to date him, and I understand that. If you want
to travel all over the world, then you probably need a
self-employed, wealthy man. I am talking from a man's
side and saying that he needs a career that he is happy
about and that this gives him his self-worth.

If he doesn't have said career??

What does Miss Intuition say?

Yes. She says—Dump his ass.

Basic 103: Date happy. Never date a depressed man.

This is a big one, ladies. You didn't sign up to be his shrink,
caretaker or Mom. Relationships are tough enough to
handle, do you really want to date a depressed, negative
soul? A guy that always feels sorry for himself or feels he
is the victim? This is an attention-seeker who will always
need something from you and will rarely reciprocate to
meet your needs.

You may feel sorry for him, but I call this man an asshole! Most know exactly what they are doing and they
prey on "women that feel sorry for them." Say boohoo to
this big pussy and then dump his ass.

I understand if you're in a long, committed relationship and something happens along the way—I get that. But to take on a man that has lost his way only because he is attractive, and you figure you can fix him? Fuck that road. That road is called, "The Highway to Hell" and you don't want to turn off there.

Instead, the basics tell us to date an upbeat, positive man. A man that thinks the world is "half full" will be a much better choice. He will lead you to a life of happiness instead of bringing you into his life of misery. This type of guy will also be able to pull himself up (and you) by his bootstraps when life throws him (or you) a curve ball.

Save your nurturing instincts for kids—with the RIGHT man, not a depressed man.

What does Miss Intuition say?

Yes. She says—He is an asshole—Dump his ass.

Basic 104: Limited baggage.

We all have our baggage. I get that. But let's give you a fighting chance of surviving the relationship. You don't need to choose this type of man anymore. Why? Because you have followed my advice and you have become a woman of value. And, because of this, men are now attracted to you. So now you have an ABUNDANCE of men to choose from that don't HAVE unnecessary baggage like below.

Too much to handle:

- Just out of a major relationship
- Is being harassed by his ex or other women

- Has six kids under the age of 10

- Shows clear signs of having addictions

- About to move to another city, town or country

- A total mommy's boy

- Wants to borrow money from you right out of the gate

- Has a felony record and/or criminal convictions

- Your friends/family/Mom hate him

- Has a personal hygiene problem

- Conceited and selfish

- Is always on porn sites

- Has anger issues

- Your dog hates him

- His own dog hates him

- Threatens you or anyone else

- Drives like a fucking idiot

- Hates/mistreats animals

- His own decent family hates him

- He has no friends

- Or any number of these put together

Am I being overly critical? Some of you probably think I am. If you do, than you need to re-think what EXACTLY you want out of a man and HOW you want to be treated. I'm here to say that you need to raise your standards. Any one of the issues above can lead to disaster. Some may seem harmless—a total mama's boy, for example. I might say the same if I hadn't witnessed the carnage of marriages falling apart because a man chose Mom every time over his wife!

Oh, and what's a little porn? Porn has become a MAJOR addiction in this world and it rarely gets addressed. Porn is so easy to escape into that many men have replaced real sex and intimacy for virtual sex and intimacy. Beware!

What does Miss Intuition say?

She says—**Dump his ass!!!!**

In Summary

Relationships are a compromise. But we don't compromise on the **basics**. We compromise on movie choices, politics, tidiness and the fact that one partner may be an extrovert while the other is an introvert. These are FUN compromises and they help us grow and love. Please understand the difference and save yourself from the emotional (and maybe physical) torture that is guaranteed to come from a person on the list above. You will also waste precious time in your life and get a chunk of your self-esteem taken away.

Raise your standards!

Every time you meet a new man have this list ready to go! If you are asking the right questions and taking him on revealing dates, you should know in two dates what type of guy you are dealing with. Go to the *"Is He the One?"* chapter for more explanation on what dates to take him on.

Also remember, you have choices and abundance of men in your life now. You don't need to pick off this list. Your new list comes from meeting men that have attended your new hobbies. Remember?

#14: Single? Power Date

You now understand men. So where else can we find quality men that have all the basics? I mentioned hobbies above, which will be your first offensive choice. But we have another.

Do you want multiple men lined up at your door telling you how awesome you are? Want to choose which one is right for you as if you were picking out baby German Shepherd pups at the shelter?

Online Dating

Yes, I said it. This is the way of the world, so don't fight me on this one. And don't tell me you tried it and you found "all creeps." You just didn't know HOW to go about it.

I have a Best Selling Amazon book written for YOU on this subject that I am going to GIVE you for FREE called, *Love is in The Mouse.*

Email me at TheSeductionGuide@gmail.com and put NOTALLMENSUCK in the subject line—I thought that might be fun :)—and I will send it out for free. Please, all I ask is that you be kind enough to READ the book. To give it out for free costs me money, so please be serious and only get it if you are going to read it. And if you want to give this or any of my books a review, I would greatly appreciate it!

This book covers everything—your profile, pics, screening out the losers, being safe and going on the date…it's all there and it's NOT some cheap ass report—it's the REAL DEAL.

Ok. So now I can talk about WHY you need to power date multiple men through online dating. Think of online dating as a tool to fill your bucket (or coy pond) with men. That's all. You go in with all the advantages. Guys outnumber women by four to one and many sites are free for women.

But here are the REAL advantages:

1) You stay busy

2) You become aloof because you have multiple options

3) You can't concentrate on one guy so you can compare all

4) You get to experiment with guys that you wouldn't normally date

5) You get free meals—Italian, Thai, Sushi—ha!

See what is happening here? I am forcing you to become a woman that is attractive to men by default. Guys want what they can't have and they CRAVE a challenge. I've made you their bait!

"Great, Gregg, please tar and feather me too!"

No, really, they think you are their bait but, in reality, THEY are YOUR BAIT!

You have me as your wingman!

By dating multiple men, your time becomes valuable and this gives you self-worth. This also makes men step up their game and realize that you are not an easy catch. Men don't like to be in competition with other men! You don't need to say that you have other choices, but you should hint. Furthermore, after the knowledge gained in this book, the losers, users, addicts and abusers will step away and look for easier targets.

Assholes need not apply.

Now you have men to compare. I get so many emails from women trying to "fix" the one man they are with. You can't "fix" a man. Now you have abundance of men to choose from. You have backups in the wings, so you are protected emotionally if one man doesn't take interest in you.

We are talking dating here. We are NOT sleeping with anyone. We are testing the waters and exposing you to variety that you have not seen before. I want you to go on dates with guys that you wouldn't ordinarily go out with. It's JUST a date. You may be surprised!

Even through my screening process, you will run into some assholes. This is good because you will learn just how EMPOWERING it is to WASTE an asshole! You will be in a public setting and if a guy gets rude you say:

"Excuse me while I go to the ladies room."

Then walk out the fucking front door! Next day, block the prick from the site you met him on.

Then FEEL how empowering this is!

You will meet some ugly ducklings too. These guys will worship you—LET THEM. And see how great it feels. Let that confidence bubble to the top of your brain and springboard you into a more confident woman.

It's YOUR time to turn the tables on men and think about YOU!

Don't tell me that you feel sorry for some of these guys. How many guys tried or succeeded to use YOU?

Remove your nurturing qualities and save them for the puppy shelter and when you have kids.

These are experiences you need so you can see HOW to deal with men. Slowly you start to VALUE your time and understand how AWESOME you really are. You start to realize what you need from a man in the way he treats you.

You have comparison.

You are in control.

You are going to meet some great guys. Trust me. This is where they go now…online! And you are in control.

Let's say you are tired of dating cheap losers without jobs. Easy! When a guy emails you, tell him you prefer a formal dinner date instead of coffee at Starbucks. If you get crickets back, SNAP, you just weeded out a cheap loser living in his Mom's basement.

The dating sites are getting more and more targeted too. You can find religious men, men with money, older men, men living on farms and Christian men, to name a few.

#15: Is He the One?

You are dating multiple men, you have sifted out the losers and one or two are starting to get your heart throbbing. But you have been here before and you have gotten your heart broken!

How can you be sure?

HIS ACTIONS!

Guys will do anything for sex. They will lie, buy you things, move in with you and even get you a ring. They will advance the relationship just enough to keep you happy and keep him happy while driving to your hoop.

Hell, I know a girl that can't get her man to marry her even though they are engaged and been living together for seven years.

Ladies, there is only one thing that counts:

How he treats you.

Forget the handsome looks, fast car and chiseled body. Go see a Chippendales show for that. If you want a REAL man that you can fall in love with, then it's ALL about how he treats you.

Date ugly? No! Go after tall, dark and handsome if you want, but don't FALL for him unless he treats you the way YOU want to be treated.

STOP! Write down how you want to be treated. Start with the sentence: *I need a man who will…?* Give me at least 10 sentences explaining exactly how you need to be treated.

I need a man who will:

- Show up when he says he will

- Never cheat on me

- Who is chivalrous and respectful of me

- Treat my kids and family like they were his own

- Show me off to his friends and family

- Put me over his friends

- Never get addicted to drugs, porn or gambling

- Honor my career

- Treat me with romance often

- Communicate his feelings instead of hiding them

- Lick me from head to toe with massive tongue

Now, obviously, it would be impossible to find them all in a man but pick 3-5 and make these NON-NEGO-TIATABLE.

Now tell yourself that you will not fall for a man until he proves he has these 3-5 traits by his **actions**.

If you don't do this, you will let your emotions take over and they will make the decision for you. DO NOT let this happen or you will get hurt.

My dick says I want to date a supermodel. But even if I can land one, will I be happy? No fucking way! My dick is my emotional brain and I won't let it take over my good sense, so don't let your emotions do it either. Find the balance in a man.

How long will it last with Mr. Chippendale? One month? Two maybe? This is why you need to know how you want to be treated and believe it—without exceptions. Vocalize it to your dates, friends and family. Men will believe you and either step up or step aside—saving you valuable time and pain.

How long will this take? I've had students that got lucky in one month! Realistically? This could take you three months to a year to find a keeper. It all depends on how picky you are and how many guys you can date per month.

See how YOU are in control now? You can design dates to test this fucker. Put him in positions and see how he reacts. It's like test driving a car without the idiot salesman next to you... its FUN! Make it fun and enjoy how empowering it feels to be the CHOOSER and not be CHOSEN.

Cast a net off your boat and fill your bucket with men. Then throw back the losers and keep a few in your coy pond. Date them, test them and see if they are tasty. If one flaps his dorsal and treats you the way YOU want to be treated, well....THIS IS YOUR KEEPER.

I don't even fish, but work with me.

Five Dates to Test Him

1) Damsel in distress.

Let's say this guy has made it into your coy pond and you have dated him a few times. On your treatment list, one of your non-negotiable items is that you want a man that will be there for you when you need him. This is what you hated about your last lazy boyfriend.

Do this:

Tell him that you need a ride somewhere because your roommate borrowed your car. Or tell him you got a leak under your sink. (I'll let you come up with something fitting.) Now see how he responds. Does he step up to the plate? Or does your text go to Mars? A good man will naturally want to "fix" the situation, if he likes you. He either fails or he gets an A. Excuses are a failing grade. Use your intuition, and be very careful if he fails two in a row.

Throw him out. Next.

2) The jealousy test.

Let's pull out another fish. This time you want a man that isn't jealous over you all the time.

Do this:

When out on a date, pretend to take a text from your ex. Tell him you can't get rid of this guy and see how he reacts. He should want to help you and "fix" the situation. See how he attempts to solve your issue. You can also take him to a sports bar and apply the same test. Wear something hot and men will be staring at your ass and making comments. Your date should have a thick skin and accept this, if he has self-worth. He should be flattered that guys are so attracted to you. But if a guy gets out of line, he should be there for your defense.

3) The family/friend test.

Accidently run into your family or show up at his. See how he interacts with your sister/Mom/brother and ask your family, later, what they thought. If you can bump into his family (accidently, of course), you can learn if he is a mama's boy or how much (if any) his family respects him. The same thing can be applied to friends. Much can be learned from these interactions. They will give you the green light forward or the red light to exit.

4) The daytime or morning date.

No guy wants a daytime or morning or even mid-week date. Why? There is no way to get into your pants! Yes, I said it and it's the truth. Only if he is WORTHY will he follow through with this type of date. You can damn well bet men are pushing to do a swan dive into your pants on a Friday or Saturday night when the lights are dim and you are drunk. Look for it and test his ass!

5) The "join my passion" date.

This is a great one because it tests his willingness to go outside his comfort zone. It tests his confidence.

Asking him to go horseback riding with you is the bomb. You can remain very comfortable while he potentially squirms. If he agrees and follows through, wow! I might date him. :)

No More Crying Over Men

If you follow my advice, you will never be sad over a man again. Think about it! You have made the decision to never fall in love with another man until he meets your criteria for treating you properly. He must prove this through his *actions*.

You will never be lied to, cheated upon, used for sex or put second to other women or men again.

Wow! Wouldn't that be nice?

It's MAGICAL. It's SIMPLE. And it WORKS!

Section 3
You Caught Him, Now Keep Him!

 #16: Keep Putting Shiny Pennies in the Jar

Jennifer asked me this question the other day:

"Gregg, everything is perfect with my man. How do I keep it this way?"

Wow. It's rare I get asked a question like this. Most men and women have problems. Either they can't find someone or they aren't happy with someone they are with. This question was quite refreshing—I have to admit.

And think about it, what good is it to follow all my advice, find and start dating a wonderful man, and then lose him because you don't have a clue how to KEEP him for the LONG run?

I have answered SOME of these longevity questions in the prior sections, but let's talk more long-term here.

First, let's answer Jennifer. I wrote this:

Hi Jenny! It's rare that I get an email saying, "Everything is perfect. How do I keep it this way?"

The bottom line is you are asking questions that NEED

to be asked. We can't control everything but you can DAMN well bet we can increase our odds of surviving to be that elusive elderly couple that remains in love after 50 years. And this is where I come in.

You are 24 going on much older and this is a tremendous advantage you have. Jon knows this. You already have many things that I teach built into you—you don't put up with addictions and you don't make a man your hobby or give up sex quickly...ALL GOOD.

The key is keeping your powers charged. Jon is going to fuck up and YOU are too at some point. The question is can you survive it? The elderly couple survived and they will be the first to tell you that it wasn't easy.

So don't SEEK perfection from Jon or yourself.

Instead, build a portfolio of experiences together that no one can match or take away. The more experiences, the better your chances of winning that furry prize on the top shelf...a loving relationship that survives the test of time.

Think about it, when 2 people travel, sail, buy a puppy together or even shit in the woods together, they build memories. And memories can keep people together for a lifetime. Even when a couple is apart for some reason, forced by travel or break up, memories can be a driving force that puts them together again.

Think of the secret to what you seek (the Holy Grail, if you will) as a giant jar of pennies. All couples start out with the same empty jar. Some couples throw shiny (good experiences) into the jar and some throw dull pennies (bad experiences) into the jar. Some throw both.

Your goal is to get as many shiny pennies into that jar and keep those dull ones out! At some point you hit the point of no return. You CAN'T break up because there is no girl that can ever replace you.

From what you have told me, you and Jon have lots of shiny copper in your jar—so keep saving!

Don't get too crazy, Jenny, you are doing great! Keep doing what you are doing and DON'T stop. Grow together, but make sure you grow on your own too.

I loved this question. And this is why I like to interact with you directly, if I can. I spend so much time dealing with problems, building people's self-esteem and other VERY important things that I tend to forget about people that are ACTUALLY happy right now and they JUST want it to continue!

And isn't the answer I gave so simple? It really is.

When you go to sleep at night and ALL your wonderful

dreams are about your man, how do you replace that? You don't want to and you can't!

That's a great way to define love and that's *"The Holy Grail"*, if you ask me.

So load up YOUR jar with shiny pennies and watch your relationship flourish.

#17: Be His Prize

This chapter is in, *Who Holds The Cards Now?* and I wanted it here too.

Remember going to the fair as a kid and hoping to win the elusive furry prize on the top shelf? You had to have it, but you could never (at least I couldn't) win the damn thing!

Become his top shelf prize.

Make him want you and only you for the rest of his life. How? Ah, glad you asked. As you may know I own a top dating advice site for men and I asked this question to thousands of men.

A **surprising** answer rose to the top:

ENTER HIS WORLD

Sounds obvious, right? But the fact is that most women don't. Sure, they might live with this man or even be married with kids, but do they really enter into their significant other's world?

My relationship flourishes today because my girlfriend and I are a team. She actively participates when I wash the car, fix things around the house or even mow the lawn. Everyday mundane chores are fun. When she grocery shops, I'll often show up with another cart and race her around the store with the goal of never stopping the cart.

These things sound silly and stupid but they are the very fabric that keeps a guy in love.

Here's why:

Couples that beat the odds are a **team**. They have become a team because they have both chosen to share common interests. If you love someone, then you love their interests too. They are the ones that, well, make most of us puke because they get along so well. They are inseparable. Like dropping off an infant at daycare for the first time, this team misses each other almost instantly. They always have each other's back, both in private and in public. A man **needs** this to fall in love and to feel validated—to feel like he is desirable, unique and very special compared to all others.

To want to participate in your man's passions doesn't mean you suck up to him or even agree with everything he says or does. It means you need to enter his world on every level. Successful couples complement each other and support each other through life without ever undermining the other. This means you accept with open arms his hobbies and passions.

Here's how:

Make an effort to understand what he really likes and why. Is it sports? Hang gliding? Cooking? Does he love the mountains? Can he build things out of wood? Or is he into German Shepherds? Ask him to teach you his hobbies and research these passions on your own. Many women go through their relationships without this key ingredient… the intertwining of hobbies with their significant other.

Don't just go shopping when he is working on his Ford Mustang—take interest and help him!

You might actually enjoy what he does. Just because he makes furniture and you know nothing about it doesn't mean that you wouldn't love to do it. Try it. Think of what you could gain: more time spent with the man you crave and a new hobby to enlighten your life. What could be better?

Not only will you see results, but he will be impressed that you **care**. This is a **huge** trait that men file into their "she could be a keeper" bin—a woman that actually wants to participate in something that he is totally passionate about. Wow!

You may say, "Why do I need to participate in his activities? He should want to participate in mine too and he doesn't."

Be the big grown-up here. A guy has his macho stupid image to keep so cut him some slack with your yoga class. Be the first to "crossover" and ask him a few questions about the difference between a safety and an extra point.

He will get so EXCITED he will shit his pants!

My girlfriend was so cute. She had no idea how football was played. But she made the chili and got involved with my bonehead friends who came over and left the toilet seat up.

I took her under my wing. Alone one day with my cat laser toy, I taught her the game. She loved it!

And from then on we enjoyed it TOGETHER. And guess what? Half the time now, we watch football together without my bonehead friends and she gets the toilet seat down. :)

You get my point. I don't mean to be sexist. I just want YOU to make the first move. And if you think like a guy, I bet you can even get us to go clothes shopping with you! Just make it a challenge and give us a reward, just like a dog, and we will go!

Watch Him Reciprocate

As a bonus, you might very well find your man asking about and wanting to participate in **your** interests. Look for this, but don't demand it. If he does, then guess what? **You** just found yourself a keeper.

A reader friend told me that his girlfriend was into this conservation program. Once a month she visited all the different streams and tributaries in her area and recorded various plant and animal life. What did he do? Without being asked, he went with her and met some new friends and eventually got very active alongside his girlfriend.

What usually happens? I think you know the answer. You go off doing things with your girlfriends while your guy watches football or works on his motorcycle. Loneliness and maybe contempt start to seed the relationship.

Instead, you could be with this guy when he is doing what he loves, and guess what? He will equate you with this love. Yes, it's psychology at work.

I know, you say you have no interest in football and motorcycles. How would you ever know? We say that we have zero interest in your veterinarian studies or your yoga class. How would we know? Stop the sexist standoff and be the first to enter his world. He has many passions (or he should) so pick one and jump in!

In Summary

Get involved with his day, his mundane chores, his work and hobbies. If he resists, dump his ass because he's not worth it. If he opens up to you, then jump in. Next, see if he reciprocates. Ask him to. If he doesn't, then you need to decide if he is still worth your time.

If he does these 2 things—you have yourself a keeper and I bow to you!

Try this one amazing tip. Enter his world and BECOME HIS PRIZE and watch the possibilities rise up before you.

#18: Change One Thing a Week

This is a great tactic to deploy to keep your man satisfied and content. If you're single, you MUST do this too. It will create confidence and make you an interesting person that ATTRACTS men. This is a major part of your new game plan!

Each week while in a relationship (or single, more coming up) change one thing per week. This will keep his interest in you at a high level all the time. Couples stagnate and they get bored, so this WORKS the BOMB!

Now I want you to use your imagination on this one. Certainly, this includes your bedroom tactics, but other things as well.

- A new haircut or a motorcycle look would be cool.

- Starting to cook brand new meals like a chef.

- Putting a leash on your cat and walking him outside would work.

- Telling him that you want to play Monopoly tonight and toast marshmallows in the fireplace.

- Reading to him if you never have before.

Just make it a REAL change. Taking off a half inch of hair does not count…we won't even notice it. But putting a pink streak in your hair for a day will shock us and make us wonder what you will do next!

Am I making any sense? Do you think I'm crazy?

THAT'S the point. We like you a little whacky and unpredictable. It keeps us excited and wanting to know what you may do next. We think that you are capable of anything! We don't need to stray because we have everything we would ever need in a woman RIGHT HERE!

Now don't go overboard. I say once a week, but you can judge best based on his reaction.

This is why it works—

Men, like you, fantasize all the time about what they don't have. We want a slut, but we want a librarian. We want an extrovert to party with, but we want an introverted shy girl to stay in with. We want a motivated woman who has a great career, but we want a lazy-ass girl on Sunday afternoons.

By changing one thing a week, you can provide all this to us in SPADES! And it's FUN too!

In the real world we get ONE color of M&M…just blue or red. CHANGE this and give us ALL the colors in the package!

Now I'll get all kinds of email saying shit like, "Gregg, you're telling me to change who I am."

NO! I'm saying role play a little and have some fun. You will be amazed how powerful this strategy can be to keep his eyes ONLY on you. We all have this capability in us. And "our craziness" usually comes out with our close friends. You act crazy with your girls SO act crazy with your man once in a while!

I teach guys this too and they have great success.

In fact, let's turn the tables for a minute.

I argue that women need several guys in their life for total happiness:

A gay guy. This is the man that you can talk to just like your girlfriends. He wants to hear all about the gossip, sex and your latest nail color. He understands when you are upset and will cry with you. You can text him five times in ten seconds and he will counter in spades.

An alpha pretty boy. This is the guy that you do the horizontal mambo with. He pleasures you. He's got the ripped abs and the broad shoulders. This man isn't the brightest bulb in the closet, but who gives a crap! He is six-foot-two with dreamy blue eyes and can carry you over his shoulder like a scarf.

The ugly old successful guy. This is the man that worships you. He will do anything for you. He provides for you. He is just happy to be a part of your life and hang around you. He tells his friends that you are his girl and you are ok with that even though you never have sex. He buys you clothes, jewelry, makes your car payment and pays for dates with the alpha pretty boy. He doesn't know about the alpha pretty boy and he will never find out.

Now I know this is a silly analogy (and sexist), but my point is that partners can be ALL these things. So using my example above, I teach men to listen to women like the gay guy, make love like the alpha pretty boy and provide (have a decent career) like the ugly old successful guy.

So, in your case, by changing things once a week or so, you BECOME a different woman to a man and you satisfy ALL his needs too. You keep him challenged and stay mysterious so he never gets bored!

Single?

Now, if you're single, you should do the same. It keeps your experiences alive! And it keeps you involved with new social circles that will expose you to quality men. I know we all have our routines that we are comfortable with. I get that. But I'm just asking for something new and different ONCE a week. If you are single, you can do this.

- Go to a new coffee spot

- Try a different place for an after work drink

- Join a new gym to workout at (get a day pass)

- Sign up for a class at your local college

- Volunteer at the local animal shelter

- Take a surf lesson

- Grag Chinese food and a comedy show with a friend

- Jump on a Carnival cruise for singles

Anything that is fresh and breaks your routine. This may also include something that does not involve social interaction, but may lead to it eventually. Reading a book on a subject that interests you is a great start that may lead to another hobby. I picked up a book on living out of an RV. I don't know if I will ever do it, but it sounds like fun and a great way to see the country. This led to me an RV show where I met some cool people.

Summary
To Date a Man,
You Must Understand a Man

Congratulations! You understand men a lot more now. I'm sure you're scratching your head wondering why you bother with us, but that's another issue! In our defense, much of how we think is society's fault.

Yeah, let's go with that. :)

By using this guide as a reference, you will be able to make much better decisions going forward. In fact, for those of you who will follow this book's advice to the "T" (I know you're out there, Sarah, Amanda, Kim from Chicago), this will be *life changing*. KEEP this book in your bedside drawer, RE-READ it a thousand times and give it to your friends!!

YOU HOLD ALL THE CARDS NOW AND THEY AIN'T SIXES—THEY'RE ACES!

You choose to be happy. In fact, right this second, if you want to be happy, you can be…try it. Make yourself happy right now by smiling or doing something stupid in the mirror. See? So if you choose to be confident or you choose to make better decisions with the guys you meet tomorrow—you can. In fact, you can start **right now.**

You might come to the realization that this so-called "man" that you are dating is an asshole and deserves to get his ass dumped because he doesn't even meet "the basics", as we discussed in chapter 13. You see, now *you are empowered with all the tools you need* to understand the male mind, build your confidence and choose quality men. What you do with these tools is your decision.

I know what I would do with them.

I gave you a TON of information so let's tighten things up in a nut shell.

Quick Review of SECTION 1—Understanding Men:

- You learned why we are like we are by examining our conveyer belt to manhood—our upbringing.

- You learned that we love and show love in a different, non-emotional ways. We protect and provide.

- Chapter 3 helped us understand the difference between what men consider "keepers" and "rest stops".

- We then covered what men require to keep happy—make them feel special, let them be in control and stand by their side.

- Next came the 5 mistakes that cause men to disappear for seemingly no reason.

Review of SECTION 2—Your New Game Plan:

- We talked about the need and power of controlling

your emotions at times, with examples.

- Then we got into *Man Mode*. This is powerful and should be re-read.

- You learned how to become an interesting person and why it is so attractive to men.

- Baggage handling came next and we discussed how you tell men about your past (and find out about theirs).

- Next you learned my formula for attraction:
  Get Busy = Build Confidence = Lure Quality Men.

- Physical improvement had to be covered—it's not just about a nice body, it's psychological too.

- You learned my unorthodox way of "shocking confidence into you." Hey, it might work!

- Next we discussed assholes and the very basics that men should bring if you are going to date them—decent career, positive attitude and no police record.

- You learned the importance of "online power dating" so you have choice—free book too. Get it!

- We wrapped this section up with how to know if he is the one—and we gave you tests to make him prove it.

Review of SECTION 3—You Caught Him, Now Keep Him

- You learned the power of experiences (shiny pennies)

and why they are the key to a lasting relationship.

- Next was the importance of joining a man in his hobby. Not to be confused with making him your hobby.

- And finally, we concluded with the power of changing one thing a week to keep a man interested in you by staying mysterious and exciting.

That's it. And I still have so much more to tell you, but I felt more stuff would be too much information to absorb in one book. But maybe that is just the man's brain talking—you probably could have handled it.

Author Bio

Hi, I'm Gregg.

I'm one of Boston's top dating coaches. I'm a little crazy (maybe a lot), I break rules, I get bored easily and I help girls and guys get a clue.

I won't bore you with my professional bio. Instead, I think you would prefer to hear the story of how I became a dating coach and what makes me qualified to write so many books and coach you.

The irony is that I came from a highly dysfunctional family. I saw my parents crumble before my eyes at an early age. Flying dishes seemed normal in my household. I came out a bit angry and proved it with 12 years of failed relationships.

But I started seeing positive things in my life too. I saw that couple, that elusive elderly couple holding hands in the park at the ripe old age of eighty. And it gave me hope! I am a problem solver and I can solve anything (I thought)…except relationships, damn it!

After a long stretch of being single, in 2009 I had an epiphany. I WANTED ANSWERS TO LOVE. I decided to study my failures and interview as many single people and couples as I could. I needed to find the secret to FINDING the right person and making it last. And do you know where I started? You guessed it, those elusive elderly happy couples!

Since then, I've talked with thousands of couples—happy couples, unhappy couples, single people of all types and everything in between.

I went to work and my friends noticed. They actually pushed me to start a dating advice website, so I did. I started coaching guys. Now I own the top dating site for men: KeysToSeductions.com. My site has exploded.

Why? Because I give REAL dating advice that average men and women can use! Let's face it, if you have GQ looks or the body and face of a model, then you don't need my help.

I listen to women. They blog on my site and help us guys attract and date quality girls. Women love us too because they get a better selection of men that "GET IT!"

Today, after thousands of interviews, I have done it…I have broken the code and I am in a great relationship myself because of it. Now I want to share my findings with YOU!

Lately, I have moved into writing and coaching women. The truth is that it was a natural next step. Being completely sincere here: I love and respect women, I honestly do. I have no interest in manipulating them, nor would I ever need to. Over the years I have listened to what women have to say. I know them inside and out. My skills were honed at an early age. I just didn't know it. I was the little runt in my family—I have three older sisters and I am the youngest and only boy.

I've been doing the dating coach thing for so long now that it's safe to say I understand what gets under your skin, and what the biggest problems are with your dating lives.

I now have eleven Amazon Best Sellers, two of which are #1 Best Sellers. I am not a writer but I sure as HECK can show you how to FIND a great guy and stay happy with him for a long time!

Today I travel and teach in all the sexy playgrounds: LA, South Beach and Las Vegas. Call me "Hitch" or call me Gregg, but just call me and watch how we can transform YOUR dating life or HELP your current relationship. I don't just write best sellers—I like to talk directly to my readers and I do so as often as I can. My readers are my friends. I am humble and I want to help you.

So join me in my quest to SOLVE your dating problems and place you on a NEW and exciting path to an extraordinary relationship!

Gregg Michaelsen,
Confidence Builder.

Find more advice for women at:
www.WhoHoldstheCardsNow.com

or on Twitter:
@YouHoldTheCards

MORE BOOKS

By Gregg Michaelsen

The Social Tigress:
Dating Advice for Women
to Attract Men and Get a Boyfriend

Who Holds the Cards Now?
5 Lethal Steps to Win His Heart and Get Him to Commit

How to Get Your Ex Back Fast!
Toy with the Male Psyche and Get Him Back
with Skills only a Dating Coach Knows

Power Texting Men!
The Best Texting Attraction Book to Get the Guy

Love is in the Mouse! Online Dating for Women:
Crush Your Rivals and Start Dating Extraordinary Men

Committed to Love, Separated by Distance:
How to Thrive in Your Long Distance Relationship

Be Quiet and Date Me!
Dating for Introverts in a World That Never Stops Talking

Find them on Amazon today!

Made in the USA
Middletown, DE
14 December 2016